W9-CPE-601

# Dynamic Taekwondo

## A MARTIAL ART & OLYMPIC SPORT

A Martial Art & Olympic Sport

# *Dynamic*

# TAEKWONDO

by Kyong Myong Lee

## HOLLYM
Elizabeth, NJ · SEOUL

First published in 1995
by Hollym International Corp.
18 Donald Place, Elizabeth
New Jersey 07208 U.S.A.
Tel: (908)353-1655   Fax: (908)353-0255

Published simultaneously in Korea
by Hollym Corporation; Publishers
14-5 Kwanchol-dong, Chongno-gu
Seoul 110-111, Korea
Tel: (02)735-7551   Fax: (02)730-8192

Hardcover ISBN: 1-56591-060-5
Paperback ISBN: 1-56591-062-1
Library of Congress Catalog Card Number: 95-76493

*Printed in Korea*

# THE WORLD TAEKWONDO FEDERATION

635 YUKSAM-DONG, KANGNAM-KU, SEOUL, KOREA 135-080 Tel : (82-2)566-2505, 557-5446 FAX : (82-2)553-4728

*Dear Readers,*

*It is my great pleasure to see that our Taekwondo leaders never stop putting their effort into the development of Taekwondo movement. Certainly, publishing a textbook of Taekwondo is an excellent tool of guiding Taekwondo practitioners in the right direction.*

*I believe this book well represents Mr. Kyong Myong Lee's strenuous effort toward the enhancement and promotion of our sport. I would strongly like to recommend this book as a very helpful guideline for those who practice and learn the fastest growing sport in international sports world.*

*Sincerely,*

*Un-Yong Kim*
*President*

*Official Sport in 2000 Sydney Olympic Games*

# PREFACE

Taekwondo has been originated from a traditional Korean Martial arts, and now it takes a prominent position as an international sport and becomes one of the official sport in 2000 Sydney Olympic Games.

In recent decades, as the martial arts sport, Taekwondo contributes to improve the quality of human life since it offers a pleasure of learning the self-defense skills and distinctive characterstics, mental desciplines and philosophical behavior.

As a Taekwondo leader, I have maintained the ascetic lifestyle for twenty years since I have started in Europe and continued to study Taekwondo based on a practical behavior.

The teachings of Taekwondo are based on the oriental philosophy. This book not only introduces the overall concept of Taekwondo, but also deeply covers the oriental philosophy with describing the arts by philosophical approach. Especially, it emphasizes morality as the fundamental human relationship, breathing and "Ki", and the philosophical relationships between "Tobok" and "Tti". It also covers the Taekwondo history, spirit, basic movements and "P'umsae" which I have extensively researched at the World Taekwondo Federation and Kukkiwon.

I hope this book will be a helpful and valuable tool for all Taekwondo practitioners who love Taekwondo.

I would like to express my sincere appreciations to Master Jung Hoe Ku who contributed for the basic movement chapter and Dr. Un-Yong Kim, President and Kum Hong Lee, Secretary General of the World Taekwondo Federation for their great contribution toward the global development of Taekwondo.

Author   Kyong Myong Lee

# TABLE OF CONTENTS

[Note:The Romanization of Korean words in this book follows the officially-approved McCune-Reischauer system. In some cases, however, names of people or proper nouns are written as they are best known or as their preferred way of spelling.]

# I

# OVERVIEW
# &
# HISTORY

# INTRODUCTION TO TAEKWONDO

Taekwondo is the name of the martial art turned modern international sport which has been independently developed over about 20 centuries in Korea. The main feature of Taekwondo is that it is a free-fighting combat sport using bare hands and feet to repel an opponent.

All of its activities are based on defensive spirit since Taekwondo was developed as a defense against enemy attacks. In old days people living simple lives lacked physical fitness and their bodies became bent in their old age. Taekwondo also served to improve health, physical fitness and poise of the people practicing it.

Our belief is that Taekwondo-trained men are self-confident, not only in physical aspects but also in their mental discipline, because they have developed superior techniques for personal defense by using their entire bodies. For a Taekwondo man, his entire body is a weapon, and he is easily able to attack and beat off an aggressor with hands, fists, elbows, knees, feet or any other part of his body.

Taekwondo literally consists of three words;
Tae(태)      means a system of foot techniques.
Kwon(권)    means a system of hand techniques.
Do(도)       means the art of experiencing the ultimate being through physical and metaphysical enlightenment.

The most important fact about Taekwondo as a martial art sport is that it is not only a superior art of self-defense, but it adds remarkable bon sens to its practitioners. Self-confidence makes people generous in their attitudes toward weaker people.

They can stand equally against any opponent, but their code forbids unfair assaults or unnecessary use of force. The practice of Taekwondo gives an individual mental attitude of modesty. The virtues of modesty and generosity are fundamentally based on self-confidence.

It is obvious that healthy bodies make active and powerful. Such mental and physical self-confidence are beneficial to the mental life of individuals as well as to their families, neighbors and their nation. The result of this combination of physical and training is the cultivation of character and the discovery of the ideal path in life. The ultimate answer to what Taekwondo is can be defined as a philosophical activity through which the practitioner can attain the highest level of unity of the body, mind and spirit.

"The ultimate winner is the one who can conquer himself. Taekwondo is a fight within the self. The one who can win himself can eventually win over the opponent."

A Taekwondo p'umsae comprises various stances, each with its peculiar nature but each blending into the other. A p'umsae consists of about two dozen stances inter-connected. Blocking, punching, striking, thrusting and kicking are among Taekwondo p'umsae, and these are properly carried out with hands, fists and feet to the vital spot of the body or target at which they are aimed, and the stances accordingly change forward stance, back stance, tiger stance and horse-riding stance, etc., as the situation requires. Most typical p'umsae are T'aeguk 1~8, Koryŏ, Kŭmgang, T'aebaek, P'yŏngwon, Shipchin, Chit'ae, Ch'ŏnkwon, Hansu and Ilyŏ.

In recent years, Taekwondo has become a modern amateur sport. It has become a modern world sport with tradition and spirit of martial science maintained. It was incorporated into regular curriculum of primary schools through colleges. It became an integral part of training in the military. Taekwondo has become a major entry in the annual athletic meet. Constitution, rules, regulations, and promotion test rules were all developed to meet requirements as international amateur sport.

Propagation of the Competition Rules of the WTF[1] has been made through International Referee (IR) Seminars held 30 times and the IR Refresher Courses held 15 times, exchanges of visits and booklets under auspices of the WTF and member national associations. For the purpose of impartial judgement of competitions, the WTF is promoting the development of electronic protectors and introductions of differential scoring system. Together with this, Executive Council of the WTF set up an ad hoc committee to conduct in-depth study of Kukkiwon tan promotion procedures.

Taekwondo uniform is neither expensive nor luxurious. It is designed to fit for free body actions. It is believed that the white color of the uniform signifies the purity and origin of all colors as well as a state which can absorb any kind of learning. There are belts, i.e. black (adult), red/black (children), red, blue, yellow and white; each color designating the degree of graded proficiency possessed by the one wearing the belt.

The white belt is for the beginner and the yellow belt is worn by 9th, 8th and 7th kŭp holders. The blue belt by 6th, 5th and 4th kŭp holders. The red belt is worn by the highest 1st, 2nd and 3rd kŭp holders. The black belt is for Taekwondo experts who hold tan ranging from 1st tan to the highest 9th tan. The red/black belt is for those who hold 1st through 3rd p'um in the junior division. The Kukkiwon is authorized to conduct promotion tests and issue tan and

1) WTF : World Taekwondo Federation

p'um certificates in accordance with the regulations on promotion tests of the Kukkiwon.

Classification of Belt & Rank

| Belt | Rank | Division |
|---|---|---|
| white | — | beginner |
| yellow | 9th, 8th & 7th kŭp | kŭp holders |
| blue | 6th, 5th & 4th kŭp | |
| red | 3rd, 2nd & 1st kŭp | |
| red/black | 1st to 3rd p'um | master |
| black | 1st to 5th tan | |
| | 6th to 9th tan | grand master |

# 2 TAEKWONDO PRACTICE AND COMPETITION

## P'UMSAE

P'umsae is a serial pattern of movements that show the essence of Taekwondo spirit and the technical system of the art. It is a behavioral form training body and mind and expressing principles of attack and defense. P'umsae is a unique and scientific form of technical sequences which preserves the centuries-old traditionalism of Korea.

P'umsae must be practiced progressively according to the p'umsaesŏn. The p'umsaesŏn is a predetermined line of the movements of each p'umsae. Every p'umsae has its own philosophical connotation according to the characteristic of the p'umsae and its historical background.

P'umsae practice is an excellent way to cultivate aesthetic appreciation as well as develop the mind and body through training balance, concentration, breathing, and endurance.

P'umsae practice requires perception of each element no matter how small the factors might be, and therefore, the practitioner can attain the final goal of perfect p'umsae.

## Meaning of Each P'umsae

① T'AEGŬK 태극
This represents the most profound oriental philosophy from which philosophical views on the World, Cosmos and Life

are derived. The T'aegŭk p'umsae consists of different movements in sequence. The vital points of this p'umsae are to make exact the speed of breath and action and move the body weight properly while executing speedy actions. Thus we can fully realize the main thought of T'aegŭk.

## ② KORYŎ 고려
"Koryŏ" is the name of an ancient dynasty in the Korean peninsula. The English name of "Korea" is originated from the name of this "Koryŏ" dynasty which was famed for its cultural achievements such as Koryŏ ceramic and for the valiant spirit of its people with which they defeated the Mongolian aggression.

Koryŏ p'umsae symbolizes the high-spirited Koryŏ people.

## ③ KŬMGANG 금강
The word "Kŭmgang" has originally the meaning of being too strong to be broken. Also in Buddhism, what can break off every agony of mind with combination of wisdom and virtue is called "Kŭmgang."

The p'umsae "Kŭmgang" is named after Mount Kŭmgang, symbol of solidity. "Kŭmgang" is also analogous to "diamond."

## ④ T'AEBAEK 태백
"T'aebaek" is the ancient name of Mount Paekdu where the legendary Tangun founded a nation for the first time in the Korean peninsula some 4,328 years ago. P'umsae T'aebaek takes its principles of movement from the word T'aebaek which means being looked up to as sacred.

## ⑤ P'YŎNGWON 평원
"P'yŏngwon" means 'vast plain'. The plain is a source of sustaining the human life and, on the other hand, a great open plain stretching out endlessly gives us a feeling of majesty that is different from what we feel with a mountain or the sea. An application of the providence of the plain which is blessed with abundance and grace as well as boundless vastness into the practice of Taekwondo is

p'umsae P'yŏngwon.

⑥ SHIPCHIN 십진

"Shipchin" has the meaning of 'decimal system' which stands for a symbolical figure of 10 meaning endless development and growth in systematic order. In p'umsae Shipchin, stability is sought in every change of movements.

⑦ CHIT'AE 지태

According to the Oriental belief, all living things come from and return to the earth (Chit'ae is derived from the meaning of the earth). The earth is indeed the origin and terminal of life. Living things as well as all the natural phenomena of the earth originate mainly from the changes and the form of earth. P'umsae Chit'ae is the movement which applies these features of the earth.

⑧ CH'ONKWON 천권

"Chŏnkwon" signifies the sky. From ancient times the Orientals have always believed and worshipped the sky as ruler of the universe and human beings. The infinitely vast sky may be a mysterious and profound world of imagination in the eyes of finite human beings. P'umsae Chŏnkwon is composed of the motions which are full of piety and vitality.

⑨ HANSU 한수

P'umsae "Hansu" derived from the word 'water' is typical with its fluidity and adaptability as manifested in the nature of water.

⑩ ILYŎ 일여

"Ilyŏ" signifies oneness. In Buddhism the state of spiritual cultivation is said to be "Ilyŏ" (oneness), in which body and mind, I (subject) and you (object), spirit and substance are unified into oneness. The ultimate ideal of Taekwondo lies in this state of Ilyŏ.

    The final goal Taekwondo pursues is indeed a discipline in which we concentrate attention on every movement, shaking off all worldly thoughts and obsession.

## Classification of P'umsae

| Name of P'umsae | Number of Patterns | Number of P'um | Lines of P'umsae | Level of Training |
|---|---|---|---|---|
| T'AEGŬK | 1 Chang | 18 | ☰ | kŭp & 1st tan (p'um) |
| | 2 Chang | 18 | ☱ | |
| | 3 Chang | 20 | ☲ | |
| | 4 Chang | 20 | ☳ | |
| | 5 Chang | 20 | ☴ | |
| | 6 Chang | 19 | ☵ | |
| | 7 Chang | 25 | ☶ | |
| | 8 Chang | 27 | ☷ | |
| KORYŎ | Single Pattern | 30 | 土 士 | 2nd tan (p'um) |
| KŬMGANG | " | 27 | 山 ⊥ | 3rd tan (P'um) |
| T'AEBAEK | " | 26 | 工 工 | 4th tan |
| P'YŎNGWON | " | 25 | — –• | 5th tan |
| SHIPCHIN | " | 31 | 十 | 5th tan |
| CHIT'AE | " | 28 | ⊥ ⊥ | 6th tan |
| CH'ŎNKWON | " | 27 | ⊤ ⊤ | 7th tan |
| HANSU | " | 27 | 水 ✳ | 8th tan |
| ILYŎ | " | 24 | 卍 | 9th tan |

## KYŎKP'A

Kyŏkp'a is one of methods that is used to measure the power and speed of the practitioner by applying a variety of Taekwondo skills to boards, bricks or any chosen material with application of physical force and mental concentration.

Kyŏkp'a is one of the most mystical aspects of the Taekwondo training experience. The bodily parts that are mostly used in Kyŏkp'a are the fist, knife-hand, ball of the foot, and side blade of the foot.

There are many techniques available such as single technique, multitple techniques, standing techniques, jumping techniques, aerospinning techniques, and multiple aerial techniques.

The most critical components in Kyŏkp'a execution are technique, power, flexibility, speed, focus, and agility. Kyŏkp'a is one of the ultimate experiences of the art. It provides a strong motivation for the practitioners and spectators to further the understanding and practice the art of Taekwondo.

## KYŎRUGI

Kyŏrugi is an integral whole of Taekwondo. It is an wholistic physical activity that utilizes the muscles and the joints of the entire body. In general, Kyŏrugi is a combat activity in which two competitors stand facing each other and compete with their offensive and/or defensive techniques.

There are two types in Kyŏrugi: Mach'wo Kyŏrugi and Chayu Kyŏrugi. Mach'wo Kyŏrugi is arranged sparring that is performed in a prearranged manner utilizing the basic Taekwondo skills and applied techniques of the p'umsae. Mach'wo Kyŏrugi helps the practitioners enhance mental focus, distance control, sense of the target, timing and accuracy. There are three types of Mach'wo Kyŏrugi: Sebŏn

Kyŏrugi, Tubŏn Kyŏrugi, and Hanbŏn Kyŏrugi. Chayu Kyŏrugi is a free sparring, which requires absolute strictness in enforcing the safety rules. There are two types of Chayu Kyŏrugi: Yŏnsŭp Kyŏrugi and Shihap Kyŏrugi.

The most important factors in Chayu Kyŏrugi are agility, power, conditioning, judgement, courage, strategy, psychological elements and techniques.

Shihap Kyŏrugi is the limelight that enabled Taekwondo to be accepted as an official 2000 year Summer Olympic Games. In order to ensure the safety of the competitors, it is mandatory for competitors to wear head gear, trunk protector, forearm guard, shin guard, groin guard and breast guard. For fair judgement, an electronic score board and simultaneous scoring system are used.

**COMPETITION**

Two players, 3 rounds & 8 weight categories.

Taekwondo competition is conducted by two contestants, Chŏng (blue) and Hong (red), on 8m × 8m contest area. Only punching and kicking techniques performed on front part of the body are allowed. Kicks are allowed only when attacking the face. Hits below the lower abdomen are forbidden. All vulnerable parts of body are covered with protectors such as head gear, trunk protector, forearm and shin guards, groin guard and breast guard to prevent injuries during competition.

One match consists of three rounds of three minutes each with one-minute recess between rounds. One referee and four judges manage the match and points are considered valid when two or more judges recognize them. One effective attack obtains one point. Two times of warning penalties or one time of Kamjŏm penalty on prohibited acts is subject to deduction of one point. The winner is determined by knockout or higher points scored and in case of a tie by superiority the decision of which is based on the initiative shown during the contest.

Eight weight categories for both men and women

| Weight Category | Men | Women | Weight Category | Men | Women |
|---|---|---|---|---|---|
| FIN | -50kg | -43kg | LIGHT | -70kg | -60kg |
| FLY | -54kg | -47kg | WELTER | -76kg | -70kg |
| BANTAM | -58kg | -51kg | MIDDLE | -83kg | -65kg |
| FEATHER | -64kg | -55kg | HEAVY | +83kg | +70kg |

Apparatus Needed
- for practitioner : Uniform
- for practice and competition : Flat surface mat
- for competitors at competition : Head gear
  Trunk protector
  Forearm & Shin guards
  Groin guard
  Women's breast guard

Four weight categories for both men and women in 2000 Sydney Olympic Games

| | Weight | | | |
|---|---|---|---|---|
| Men | -58kg | -68kg | -80kg | +80kg |
| Women | -49kg | -57kg | -67kg | +67kg |

# THE HISTORY OF TAEKWONDO

## THE PRIMITIVE SOCIETY

People in primitive ages, no matter where they lived, had to develop personal skills to fight in order to obtain their food and to defend themselves against their enemies, including wild animals.

They also had to invent weapons for more effective defense and easier subsistance. However, even after they learned to use weapons, they never stopped their efforts to promote the development of their bodies and minds by practicing various games, especially in the form of religious rites.

## KOGURYŎ DYNASTY

The Korean ancestors who settled in several tribal states in this land after the neolithic age had many such activities. Yŏnggo in Puyŏ state, Tongmaeng in Koguryŏ, Much'ŏn in Ye and Mahan, and Kabi in the Shilla dynasty are some of the striking examples of the "sports activities" which ancient Koreans practiced in their religious rites. These events were developed into exercises to improve health or martial abilities.

The long experience of ancient people in defending themselves against the attacks of animals as well as their imitation of the defensive and offensive positions assumed by the animals slowly led the people to develop more effective skills of their own in the use of their hands in fighting, thus creating a primitive form of "T'aekkyŏn (an old name of Taekwondo)."

The origin of Taekwondo in this country can be traced back to the Koguryŏ dynasty, founded in 37 B.C. since mural paintings found in the ruins of the royal tombs built by that dynasty show scenes of Taekwondo practice. Muyong-ch'ong and Kakchu-ch'ong are two royal tombs built in the Koguryŏ dynasty, which were discovered by a group of archeologists in 1935. They were located in Tungku, Chain county, Tunghua province in Manchuria, where Koguryŏ had its capital in Hwando province.

The ceiling of the Muyong-ch'ong carried a painting depicting two men facing each other in Taekwondo practice, while the mural paintings of Kakchu-ch'ong show two men wrestling. In reference to this particular painting, Tatashi Saito, a Japanese historian, in the "Study of Culture in Ancient Korea," says:

"The painting either shows us that the person buried in the tomb practiced Taekwondo while he was alive or it tells us that people practiced it, along with dancing and singing, for the purpose of consoling the soul of the dead."

The construction of the above two tombs dates back to the period between 3 A.D. and 427 A.D., during which, historians say, Hwando province remained the capital of Koguryŏ. It can therefore be inferred that Koguryŏ people started practicing Taekwondo during that period.

## HWARANGDO OF THE SHILLA DYNASTY

Taekwondo was also practiced during the Shilla dynasty. Shilla was a kingdom founded in the southeastern part of the land some 20 years before Koguryŏ in the north. At Kyŏngju, the ancient capital of Shilla, two Buddhist images are inscribed on the Kŭmkang Giant Tower at Sŏkkuram Grotto in Pulkuk-sa Temple, portraying two giants facing each other in a Taekwondo stance.

Shilla was famous for its Hwarang. Korean culture and martial arts of the period were strongly influenced and enriched by the Hwarangdo, a military, educational and social organization and noble youths of the Shilla dynasty. The codes of honor upon which the Hwarang was based were loyalty to the nation, respect and obedience to one's parents, faithfulness to one's friends, courage in battle and avoidance of unnecessary violence and killing. The influence of the Hwarangdo played an important role in unifying the three kingdoms.

Many scattered descriptions in written documents of the three kingdoms such as the Samguk Yusa, the oldest document of Korean history, show that Hwarangdo not only regarded the Taekwondo practice for their unarmed combat study as an essential part of physical and military training, but also recommended it as a recreational activity.

Archeologic findings such as mural paintings on the royal tombs of the Koguryŏ dynasty, the stone sculptures of pagodas of temples produced during the Shilla period, and many scattered descriptions in written documents show that many studies of fighting stances, skills and formalized movements closely resemble the present stances and forms of Taekwondo. Therefore, it can be inferred that people in the three kingdoms practiced an art very like the one we study today.

## SUBAK IN THE PERIOD OF KORYŎ AND YI DYNASTIES

In the history of Koryŏ, Taekwondo, which was then termed "Subak," was practiced not only as a skill to improve health and as a sports activity but it was also encouraged as a martial art of considerably high value.

Here are a few extracts from the historical record of Koryŏ that testify to the popularity of Taekwondo as a martial art.

"King Uijong admired the excellence of Yi Ui-min in Subak and promoted him from Taejŏng (military rank) to Pyŏlchang."

"The king appeared at the Sang-chun pavillion and watched Subak contests."

"The king watched Subak contest at Hwa-bi place."

"The king came to Ma-am and watched Subak contests."

These records indicate that Subak in the Koryŏ dynasty was also practiced as an organized sport for spectators.

Subak is believed to have gained its highest popularity during the reign of King Uijong, between 1147 and 1170 A.D. This period roughly corresponds to the era that includes part of the Chinese Sung and Ming dynasties, during which the Chinese "Kungfu" became widely popular after this self-defense art was developed into two advanced systems, namely Neikya and Weikya. These two systems differ chiefly in that the one employs more defensive skills and the other offensive skills.

The above fact is worth noticing as it further shows that Taekwondo is not only of a pure Korean origin but it has achieved independent development throughout the long history of Korea.

What is very important about Subak in the Yi dynasty (1392~1910 AD) is that there was a book published to teach the game as a martial art and that it became more popular among the general public whereas earlier it had been to a certain degree monopolized by the military in the preceding Koryŏ dynasty.

A historical record indicates that pepole from both Ch'ungch'ŏng and Chŏlla provinces once gathered at the village of Chakji located along the provincial boundary to compete in Subak. This record supports the notion that

Subak played an important role as a popular sport activity of the people in the Yi dynasty.

Furthermore, people who aspired to be employed by the military department of the royal government were eager to learn Subak because it was included as one of the major subjects of the test to be taken by the applicants.

Meanwhile, King Chŏngjo published "Muye Tobo T'ongji," an illustrated textbook on martial arts, which included Taekwondo as one of major chapters. It is obvious, therefore, that Subak became an important national sport and attracted much attention from both the royal court and the general public during the Yi dynasty.

However, in the latter half of the Yi dynasty, the importance of Subak as a martial art began to decline due to negligence of the royal court, which was constantly disturbed by strife between feuding political factions. As a result, Subak remained merely as a recreational activity for ordinary people.

## TAEKWONDO DEVELOPMENT IN MODERN TIMES

Taekwondo in the first half of the 20th century:

Along with the deterioration of national fortunes, the fall of the military was accelerated by the dismantling of the army; finally Japanese imperialists colonized Korea through an oppressive forceful invasion. The oppression of the Korean people by the Japanese imperialists worsened, and the practicing of martial arts, which could have been used as a means of revolt, was forbidden. However, Taekwondo persisted in the spirit of the Korean people as a physical and spiritual training method of anti-Japanese organizations such as the Indepedence Army and the Liberation Army, and as a legacy which had to pass on to the younger generation.

After Liberation from the Japanese Rule to Present:

After liberation from the Japanese rule on August 15, 1945, those with an aspiration to revitalize the traditional art of Taekwondo taught their followers, and at last, on September 16, 1961, the Korea Taekwondo Association was established. On February 23, 1962, the Korea Taekwondo Association became the 27th affiliate to join the Korea Amateur Sports Association. On October 9, 1963, Taekwondo became an official event for the first time in the 44th National Athletic Meet. Taekwondo has been highlighted even in the sports festival for mankind, the Olympics. Its great leaps in the development of competition rules and protective equipment started with the 1963 National Athletic Meet 32 years ago.

Korean instructors began going abroad to teach Taekwondo in the 1960s, which could be called a turning point in the history of Taekwondo. Taekwondo made its way to the world sport through the 1st World Taekwondo Championships held in Seoul, Korea in May 1973 with participation of 19 countries. At the Seoul meet held on May 28, 1973 on the occasion of the championships, representatives of those countries established the World Taekwondo Federation (WTF).

Presently, member countries of the WTF total 145 and the global Taekwondo population is estimated at 40 million people. Spurred by the recognition of Taekwondo by the IOC at its 83rd General Session in 1980, Taekwondo has been rapidly becoming an international sport. It was adopted as a demonstration sport of the 24th Seoul Olympics held in 1988 and the 25th Barcelona Olympics to be held in summer of 1992.

The 103rd General Session of the International Olympic committee on September 4 unanimously ratified the decision of the IOC Executive Board to adopt Taekwondo as an official program of the Games of the 27th Olympiad in Sydney.

Taekwondo has consolidated its position in the world sport as fast as any other martial art sport. Besides in continental championships hosted by four member regional unions of the WTF as well as in the World and Women's World Championships, World Cup, CISM Taekwondo Championships and FISU World University Championships, Taekwondo is being played as an official sport in most of international multi-sport games such as World Games, Goodwill Games, Pan American Games, All African Games, Southeast Asian Games and Central American Games, South American Games, South Pacific Games, etc.

## REFERENCES ON TAEKWONDO'S GLOBALIZATION

WTF's Affiliation with International Sports Organizations

Oct. 1975   affiliated with the General Association of International Sports Federations (GAISF)

July 1980   recognized by the International Olympic Committee (IOC)

Jan. 1981   affiliated to the International Council of Sports Science & Physical Education (ICSSPE)

Oct. 1983   affiliated with the International Group for Construction of Sports and Leisure Facilities (IAKS)

May 1986   affiliated to the Comite Internationale pour le fair-play

Recognition of Taekwondo by International Sports Organizations

April 1976   adopted by the International Military Sports Council (CISM) as its 23rd official sport

July 1981   first participated in the World Games I as an official event

Aug. 1983   adopted by the Pan American Sports Organization (ODEPA) as an official sport of the Pan American Games and made its debut in 1987 Pan American Games in Indianapolis, U.S.A.

Nov. 1983  adopted by the Supreme Council for Sports in Africa (SCSA) as an official sport of All African Games

Sep.  1984  adopted by the Olympic Council of Asia (OCA) as an official sport of the 1986 Asian Games in Seoul, Korea

June 1985  adopted by the Executive Board of the IOC as a demonstration sport of the 1988 Olympic Games in Seoul, Korea

May  1986  adopted as a Federation Internationale du Sport Universitaire (FISU) even for World University Championships at the FISU Executive Committee meeting held in Zagereb, Croatia

Sep.  1988  first staged in the Olympic Games as one of the demonstration sports in 1988 Olympic Games in Seoul, Korea

Jan.  1990  adopted by the Central American Sports Organization as an official sport of the Central American Sports Games

Aug.  1991  adopted by the Bolivarian Directive Council as the regular program of the 1993 Bolivarian Games in Cochabamba, Bolivia

Sep.  1991  adopted as an official sport of the 3rd Goodwill Games

April 1992  adopted as an official sport of the Hiroshima Asian Games scheduled for October 2-16, 1994

Aug.  1992  staged in the 1992 Olympic Games in Barcelona, Spain as a demonstration sport Sep. 1994 adopted as an official program in 2000 Sydney Olympic Games at 103rd IOC session in Paris

## Establishment of WTF Regional Unions

Oct.  1974  1st Asian Championships held in Seoul, Korea

May  1976  European Taekwondo Union's inaugural meeting held in Barcelona, Spain on the occasion of the 1st European Championships

Oct.  1976  preparatory inaugural meeting of the Asian Taekwondo Union held in Melbourne,

Australia

Sep. 1978 inaugural meeting of the Pan American Taek-
wondo Union held on the occasion of the 1st
Pan American Championships held in Mexiço
City, Mexico

April 1979 African Taekwondo Union inauguated in Abid-
jan, Ivory Coast on the occasion of the 1st
African Championships

# II

# PERSPECTIVES ON MARTIAL ART PHILOSOPHY

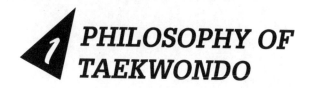

# PHILOSOPHY OF TAEKWONDO

## THE NATURE OF TAEKWONDO

The nature of Taekwondo is founded on two fundamental aspects; pracitical value and ideological value. The practical value of Taekwondo is found in the elemental movements of each individual technique and in the principles governing those movements. The ideological value of Taekwondo is found in the three ideals which from the identity of Taekwondo: the technical ideal, artistic ideal, and the philosopic ideal. Further, modern Taekwondo is a method of Physical Education and a system of competition.

### The Technical Ideology of Taekwondo

The technical expression of Taekwondo originally derived its value from the practical aspects of training. Bare-hand self-defense and physical exercise for health were the basic practical benefits of Taekwondo.

Therefore, the technical ideal of Taekwondo was seen as the practical application of training and techniques to human living conditions. Even as an awareness of Taekwondo's other ideals emerge, the technical ideal remains an essential element of Taekwondo training. The technical ideal, then is embodied in the word "Musul" which describes its practical values.

## The Artistic Idelology of Taekwondo

Art arises from a state of mind and soul in union and is expressed through an action consistent with that union. When one devotes mind and soul to the refinement of Taekwondo skill, a sensation of exquisite achievement can be realized outside of the practical considerations of technical development.

The sublimation of practical concerns into the desire to develop complete and perfect Taekwondo skills is the concept of "Muye," the artistic ideal of immersion of soul in body for the sake of perfection of action.

## The Philosophic Ideology of Taekwondo

The concept of "to(道)" is the central metaphysical concept which covers the entire realm of oriental philosophy.

The philosophic ideal of Taekwondo training is the realization of the relationship between man and nature or the universe as discovered through practicing, and how to live in harmony with that universe. This is the essence of "Muto."

A narrow sense of normative concepts such as "courtesy" and "sense of honor" have little to do with Taekwondo's philosophic ideal. Nor is this ideal found in Technical values such as p'umsae or the concept of a "deathblow." The philosophic ideal is moving away from an introverted mind toward an extroverted mind.

## The Nature of Taekwondo as Physical Education

Physical education is the systemized attempt to integrate man's intelligence, emotion, and will through physical action. Taekwondo's technical, artistic and philosophic ideology abound with educational values.

Developing the physical body is the domain of technique,

developing a concentrated spirit the domain of art, and achieving a harmony between mind and body as well as an understanding of, and cooperation with nature is the realm of Taekwondo philosophy. The philosophic objective of perfecting the human being through Taekwondo is identifiable to the philosophic objectives of physical education thus defining Taekwondo as a methodology of physical education's principles.

Taekwondo had not been altered or exploited as a "new," modern form of physical training, but instead has always embodied the values of physical education.

The essential values of Taekwondo which begin to be formed through the technical ideal at the inception of training and which come to maturity at the philosophic or "to(道)" stage correspond with the nature of physical education which exists to develop an ideal human being through a physical training regime.

## The Nature of Taekwondo as a Competition

Competitions of strength are an expression of man's natural instincts. Historically, competitions of strength between men have been the most common of all competition patterns. The nature of Taekwondo's development as a form of competition has been that of a competition of strength which relies on skill for its proper expression.

Man naturally desires to prove that he is superior to his opponent in competition, this desire combined with the resultant values derived from sincere efforts to develop technically and the human interaction of training and competitive confrontation all shape the Taekwondo competition. These experiences and lessons together with other factors such as sportsmanship, i.e., human responsibility, as well as pleasure and recognition have led to the development of the concept of Taekwondo competition. Historically, Taekwondo developed as a "hoe" or game, therefore, Taekwondo as a martial art has a historical relationship with the values of competition.

The competitive ideals of Taekwondo are power, quickness, and accuracy. The embodiment of these ideals in the training and competition process gives Taekwondo its unique identity as a modern sport.

## THE SPIRIT OF TAEKWONDO

### The Meaning of Taekwondo Spirit

Spirit and mind are two words often confused in usage because of their similarity. However, spirit refers to the immaterial intelligence which systematically establishes human thinking on the basis of value. Therefore Taekwondo spirit means the Taekwondo man's systematic thought process in regarding values established through Taekwondo training.

When one reaches an improved ability to perceive the relative merit of things and act effectively and decisively as a result of training, then it can be said that Taekwondo spirit has been, to some extent established, and embodied. Not until a behavioral and moral philosophy have been established as a consequence of internal assimilation of the three dimensions of Taekwondo ideology, i.e., technical, artistic, and philosophical, can it be said that a comprehensive Taekwondo spirit has been established.

### Technique and Spirit

Technique is the starting point as well as the ultimate goal of Taekwondo. All the intrinsic values of Taekwondo arise from technique and exit at any stage of development within and because of technique.

Taekwondo spirit therefore, starts with technique, develops itself within technique and arrives at perfection through technique. As one trains in a series of techniques which develop progressively from basic movements, p'umsae and kyŏrugi to higher levels, spirits is likewise developed progressively and in concrete stages.

The determinant factor in Taekwondo training is called the reactive motion. Man, existing in a certain environment, is influenced by that environment and in turn, acts against the environment. The medium through which each influence the other is the reactive motion. Practice of Taekwondo goes from reactive training in a primary field of environment in which an opponent is initially encountered, through a broader field in which the opponent is engaged, to the final field in which an absolute and infinite awareness of the environment is attained by transcending the opponent's awareness of the environment.

If that awareness can be reached, no gap would exist between the state of an individual's internal consciousness and that of the external environment, and it would become possible for the individual to control and adjust the internal and external fields subjectively.

This type of development of the spirit is accomplished by pure immersion of spirit into a technique and through the experiences and awakening within that technique. During fierce Kyŏrugi of other confrontations, one's composure is not lost, the self and the opponent are both deeply and calmly viewed within the mind, action is neither feared nor avoided, all external concerns about result of outcome are discarded.

This is the specific description of the above mentioned ultimate stage of spirit.

## Putting Taekwondo Spirit into Practice

Taekwondo spirit refers to the mental frame of the ideal human being into which Taekwondo training seeks to develop. It is a mental image of the ideal Taekwondoist which any trainee carries.

When the three dimensions of Taekwondo, i.e., technique, art and philosophy are integrated holistically to form another dimension of human personality, it is seen as the beginning of actualizing Taekwondo spirit.

Taekwondo has a system of value built around two axes; martialism and morality or "to(道)."

Taekwondo cultivates the spirits's energy through the rituals of training and through "to," and attempts to integrate them into one. The product of that union is called "chong(正)" or propriety. Contained in this concept is the "chong(浮)" referring to a clean heart and "chong(征)," referring to intrepidity, and finally "chong(定)" of restraint.

Ultimately then, Taekwondo in the form of education, sport, or humane personification (or "to") seeks a practical philosophy based on a martial morality which gives man a way to think and act with propriety recognized as an intrepid, altruistic human being.

## THE SPIRIT OF COMPETITION

As in the Olympic slogan of "Faster, Higher, and Stronger," Taekwondo competition encourages competitors to improve the level of human capacity. Taekwondo competition is a form of education that takes place through the practice of skills and their application in competition, based on traditional values. The fundamental significance of Taekwondo competition lies in the fact that the competition ring provides a venue where following the rules and doing one's best are rewarded. The site of competition is a place to learn the way to achieve harmony and perfection of the mind, body and spirit through the discovery of true self. This is possible through the struggle within self and against the opponent.

Competition is a method of developing the full potential of the human body, both physically and technically. Taekwondo competition pursues the development and integration of fitness, technique and strategy as well as a sense of humility and sportsmanship.

The ultimate ideal of Taekwondo practice is to achieve a state of mind in which the performer is acutely aware of the endlessly changing competition environment and can effortlessly react to such changes. This state of mind becomes possible through the mastery of a broad range of offensive and defensive Taekwondo skills.

# PHILOSOPHICAL CHARACTER OF TOBOK

In the beginning of Taekwondo training, the practitioner encounters the tobok and learns ettiquette from the Sabŏmnim. The tobok is a special clothing for training the mind and body in which the spirit of Korea and the centuries-old tradition is alive. So it is called a "handobok."

The tobok consists of trousers, upper garment and belt, of which is called "hanbul." The tobok has a similarity with traditional Korean clothes "hanbok." The origin of the hanbok is not known. There are, however, records that shows the use of costumes in the period of Shilla (Samkuk Sagi), Kaya (Samkuk Yusa), and Koguryŏ-Paekche-Shilla periods (Sasŏ, China). It is written in the "Koryŏ Tokyŏng" by Sukyŏng of Early China that "People in the Koguryŏ Kingdom wear white costumes with black silk belts around the waist."

It seems that the white costumes could be daily clothes for the Koguryŏ people. It also seems that the long upper garment and trousers must have been the same type of cloth that were found on the wall paintings in the tombs of the three kingdoms.

Taekwondo tobok which is similiar to the traditional Korean clothing in the method of making, has three kinds of shapes: circle ( ○ ), square (□), and triangle (△). The waist line of the uniform is circular shape, the cuffs square and the hip area triangular. The upper garment is made according to the same manner.

How to fold the Tobok

It seems that tobok which is quite different from common clothing has a tradition of conservatism, and therefore, it is reasoned that the tobok that Kokuryŏ people used to wear must be quite similiar to the one that people during the Tangun-chosŏn used to wear (BC 37-AD668). It also seems that Ch'oesŏnin of Kokuryŏ and Kuksŏn-hwarang of Shilla were from the same tradition of Tangun-Chosŏn, and that Kukjarang of Tangun-Chosŏn became the Ch'oesŏnin of Kokuryŏ and Hwarang of Shilla.

"Won( ○ )" symbolizes the heaven, "Bang(□)" the earth, and "Kak(△)" the man. The circle denotes the heaven, the square the earth and the triangle the man. The three symbols are the foundation of the universe (Samilshingo). The traditional Korean costumes are made based on the three symbols, and the symbols transform into the unity of the three called "han."

The numeric concept of the Ch'ŏnbugyŏng, which contains the principles of the heaven as one, the earth as two, and the man as three, brought the complete theoretical background for the formation of the traditional Korean costumes. From these conclusions, it can be reasoned that tobok has the same historical records of transformation as the traditional Korean costume has had. According to the theory of the "Yin" and "Yang", the man is the small universe, trousers which is Yin the earth, upper garment which is Yang the heaven, and belt the man himself, which stems from the spirit of Samjae. The spirit of Samjae, which explains the principle of the heaven, the earth, and the man, applies to the every aspect of the life of Koreans including in the production of all different sorts of costumes.

Tobok and hanbok have the form of no beginning and no ending and it is quite difficult to conclude that the methods of making them were designed by one person's idea. There is some historical proof that shown the history. One example is from the article of the Chosŏn Daily Newspaper on the day 18th of April in 1990. It says that a Japanese female professor discovered a 400 year old Ch'ŏnik Chollae P'um – male costume used during the period of Chosŏn dynasty.....found as an original shape.....seems booty.....given by the Shogun Poongshin..

At the beginning the tobok were made only in white color. In 1970, the division was made between the uniform for the under black belt and the black belt. The tobok has a V-neck shape. The p'um uniform has red-black stripes along the neck and the tan uniform only a black stripe.

The white color in the uniform symbolizes the background of the universe. According to the philosophy of the Korean tradition, the origin of the universe is the oneness which pronounced in Korean as Han. Han stems from the color of white. The white is the essence of the universe in Korean belief.

The reason of the V-neck is to reduce the uncomfortableness of the previous traditional uniform which would be loosen too often during the practice. The V-neck uniform looks neat and is convenient to wear.

Tobok is not only a costume for daily practice in Tojang but also a competition cloth for national level as well as the Olympic Game. The philosophical significance of the tobok is in keeping it clean and having proper respect and ettiquette toward it.

# PHILOSOPHICAL SIGNIFICANCE OF THE BELT "TTI"

In every day life, belt is addressed as hŏritti or yodae (meaning waist belt).

In the dichotomy of the human body of head, waist and legs, waist is at the center of the three. Tying the belt means the will power to organize the self and apperance.

In Taekwondo practice, tti (belt) is a necessary part along with upper garment and trousers. It is a part of a trinity of the jacket, pants and the belt. Ttis are divided into three categories for the level of the achievement as uniforms are, such as color belt, p'um belt (red-black), and black belt. The concept of the trinity in the Eastern philosophy is the most fundamental in the belief of the universe, which they regard as being composed of the heaven, earth and people. It is the source of all life. The trinity concept is the essential part of Ch'ŏnbugyŏng. Most of all, Koreans regard people as the most valuable.

The example of the philosophy is in the Taekwondo uniform. The upper garment of the uniform equals the heaven: the trousers the earth: the belt the person. A person, in Korean belief, is a micro universe.

Tti has five colors: white, yellow, blue, red and black. The primary colors are yellow, blue and red. The white and black are from the philosophy of Yin (Ŭm) and Yang:

How to tie the tti

meaning the sun and moon, day and night, beginning and ending. The meaning of the five colors can be found in the theory of Ŭm-yang Ohaeng Sŏl. Ŭm-yang has been understood as the ultimate principle of cosmic order that enables production of all life forms that act and react. Ŭm-yang O-haeng Sŏl consists of the theory of Ŭm-yang that explains the harmony of Yin (Ŭm) and Yang, and the theory of O-haeng Sŏl that describes the birth and death of all lives through interaction of the five components such as fire, water, wood, metal and soil. And the north, south, east, west and center are called Obangsaek. In the human body, the five elements are equal to heart, kidney, lung, liver and spleen. The five colors in the Taekwondo uniform are based on the principle of Ohaeng-ogi. These colors are widely used in Korean lives in design, construction and clothes.

Taekwondo tti system starts from the 9th kŭp and ends at the 9th tan. Nine is the sum of the five components, the heaven, the earth, Yin and Yang. The kŭp system in Taekwondo descends from 9 to 1 whereas the tan system ascends from 1 to 9. This system stems from the eastern belief that all life forms descend from the heaven, live on the earth, return to where they came from. In the decimal systim, 9 is also the highest number.

The Taekwondo system is designed according to the principle of Ohaeng. Practitioners can develop the internal ki (energy) through the process of collecting and dispersing energy within the body. The five different energy formats (ogi), then, can be developed. The ki is the spring of a constant new life source.

In tying the belt around the waist, the two ends meet, after two rounds, at the center of the stomach called Tanjŏn. Then the belt will make triangle shape to complete the knot. The shape of the triangle denotes the oneness of a person. The meaning of this ceremonial process is to collect all energy within and without into the Tanjŏn so that the practitioner can utilize the ki in the application of techniques.

Traditionally, Tojang means the place of awakening. That is pollible by practicing the collecting and dispersing the energy freely through techniques, developing the inner energy to creat harmony and order, arriving at the awakened self, and finally attaining the enlightenment – the big meeting with the big self.

It is essential for Taekwondo students to take special care of the uniform. The practice requires strict order, and the order comes from the respect of the seniority of the belts. The more respect the practitioner has to the significance of the belt, the more serious he/she becomes toward the training of the art. That will consequantly lead him/her to the bigger self-enlightenment.

A beginner begins from a white belt. The white color in Korean history has a great significance. When Tangun, who was the son of Hwanung, founded Korea under the name of Chosŏn, the name was based on the spirit of worshiping the sun (symbolizing brightness). White color means birth or begining (the ultimate source). It is the cental color of the three primary colors and a base of all. That connotes the beginning as well as the end which is another beginning of a new start: everlasting recurrence of life and death.

Yellow symbolizes a new birth, blue rebirth, red passion, and black completion. The five belt colors show the regorous process of practice and finally arriving at the completion of the big-self.

The belt system in Taekwondo training has a significance not only in the philosophical comprehension of the art, but also as a way of life. It can never be overemphasized how important it is to cultivate proper etiquette to accomplish the ultimate goal of training the art of Taekwondo.

# III

# THEORETICAL ASPECTS

# 1 TAEKWONDO AND THE THEORY OF POWER

## MUSCULAR POWER

The power of the human body comes from muscular activity. The force that is generated by the muscle is called muscular power. Muscles make force when they contract utilizing the energy that is generated by the fibrous reactions.

Physiologically, power means muscular power. There are two types of muscles: smooth and striated. Smooth muscles are used for involuntary functions of the body. Striated muscles are used for voluntary contractions. Striated muscles are made of two types of fibers: slow twitch and fast twitch.

In Taekwondo training, the power of techniques such as striking, punching and kicking are to be shown at the moment of the impact. The degree of the impact is decided by the muscular power and speed. Therefore, to increase the attacking power the speed and weight must be increased.

Taekwondo techniques utilize mostly the fast twitch muscles. The power of each technique can be enhanced by proper exhaling at the moment of the impact. To strengthen the fast twitch muscles it is essential to breathe out during the excution of the technique. In other words, Taekwondo practice requires the efficient use of the muscles and the theory of the power. For example, when you punch to the trunk, you can make more power by transmitting the whole bodily force through the fast twitch muscles in the arm rather than just depending on the force of the arm itself. The other important point in the execution of the punch is that you must relax the shoulders. It is quite difficult to integrate the total bodily force when the punch is traveling horizontally while the upper body and lower body is sustained vertically. By relaxing the shoulders, you can reduce the burden to the axle, therefore the fists can move fast. It is very common that you hear from instructors in Taekwondo schools to free your shoulders if you want to create maximum power.

## FOCUS OF POWER

The principle of focus is in utilizing the resistance of gravity that works against the technical exertion of the body. The bodily force comes from three sources: elasticity of the leg muscles, of the stomach and back muscles and of the arm muscles. When all of these three components are integrated, maximum power can be generated.

The use of the arm and leg is our free will. Punching and kicking take place at our own free will of the mind. The will of the mind is the one that directs our body. The focus of physical power is only possible by focusing the mind that is the cause of the activities. The concept of the focus and will in Taekwondo training is included in the general concept of the mind.

The final goal of Taekwondo training is not only in developing the physical being and technical perfection but more in the achievement of the harmony of mind and body. Therefore, in every technical execution must be the existance of the mind. The mind or the spirit is the higher concept that enables the body to move. Every Taekwondo skill must be channeled properly by the controlled manner of the mind and be geared toward the unity of the being. Maximum power only comes when the oneness of the mind and body occurs.

## KI (BREATH CONTROL)

The life form of the human being is maintained by some
sort of the energy. In Taekwondo training, ki is the source
of energy. The ki can be developed by Tanjŏn Hohŭp.
Through the Tanjŏn Hohŭp, you can experience the exis-
tence of ki and make use of the energy to control your
mind. In our daily conversation, we often hear the word of
"Shimgi."

At this time, shim means the mind and ki means the energy. The shim is in constant tranquility (chŏng 靜) but the
ki is constantly in motion (tong 動). In Taekwondo training,
the shim and the ki must be unified as one. When the
proper ki is understood and practiced, it is not impossible
to have super human power. That is the reason for such a
long history and mysticism on the concept of the ki in the
martial art society.

# TAO, THE WAY: PHLOSOPHICAL APPROACH

"Tao" or "to (道)" is a term that can be found in most martial arts that are practiced in the Eastern societies. It is an essential word in Eastern philosophy and the key element in Taoism, which stems its origin from the third or fourth centuries. That seemed to answer the yearnings of men of feeling and imagination for a vision of the eternal where they could forget the chaos of the present. The character tao means the way of the course of nature.

The word tao appears initially in the book of "Tao Te Ching" by Lao Tzu. He thought tao is the origin and beginning of the cosmos. Tao is the metaphysical absolute being that transcends time and space. He said, "If you can speak of, it's no more tao." Han Hsi-tsai said, "Tao is the source of all being and the secret prescription of all matters."

Then, where does the origin of the tao begin? To answer this, it is necessary to carefully examine the structure of the Chinese and Korean characters. In the Chinese character of tao, it consists of two connotations: road and head. Put in a different translation, road means walking and head thinking. Walking means action and thinking means philosophical being. Therefore tao is a action philosophy.

In Korean word of "to(道)", the word has the same root of the characters of "topta," which means helping. Therefore, it can be translated as "to is giving and receiving help," which means all beings in the universe are in the relationships as such.

In many books on Taoism, it is emphasized that tao is necessary to keep our world in order. Without it, it is called non-tao, in which hurting and killing other life can easily take place. Therefore, when tao is prevailing, the world is in balance, whereas when non-tao appears, crimes and unbalance of society prevail.

From these retrospectives, it is manifested that the origin of the Korean philosophy that has the root in the spirit of Tangun who is the founding father of the nation, has a great significance in explaining the concept of tao. The essence of Tangun's philosophy was Hongik Ingan, which means "The rising of wholistic humanity." The practice of the Hongik Ingan is only possible through helping as many others as he/she can. The Korean concept of the tao must be based on the Tangun's Hongik Ingan. It inspires the spirit of humanism for the benifit of all. Koreans have tried to preserve humanity through the practice of these concepts.

It is of course quite impossible to define the tao in words. There have been innumerable definitions of tao, and yet, none can describe tao correctly.

"To(道)" in Taekwondo(跆拳道) roots the basis of the concept of humanism. It is a traditional martial art which has been influnced by Tangun's philosophy, Confucianism, Buddhism, and Taoism.

Eastern philosophy has the fundamental ground on the spirit that human mind and body are not a separate entity, rather it is a oneness. By the same token, when you practice Taekwondo, you train the body and mind in order to achieve the oneness of both. The martial artistic view of Taekwondo is ultimately the realization of the oneness of the mind and body, and the oneness of the activity and non-activity. In other words, the harmony with nature allows the self to merge with the tao, and the merging to acchieve the great mission of acomplishing one's happy life.

Therefore, Taekwondo training must start from meeting the tao and end in the tao. The "to" in Taekwondo is a natural course of human action. If Taekwon is bodily activity, to is metaphysical activity. If Taekwon is a general behavioral conduct, to is the insight and intuition. That is the dualistic aspect of Taekwondo: internal and external concepts.

Through Taekwondo training, the practitioner can enhance the self from averageness to excellence. "To" in Taekwondo leads us to integrate all efforts in training for the unification of energy into the unity of the mind and the body to achieve the most desirable character.

"To" is a philosophical insight into the physical activity utilizing the bodily parts through everyday practice, competition, and etc.

Taekwondo is a Korean martial art that develops the mind and body to be a wholistic human being through progressive exercise programs by improving the ability of concentration, insight into the self and harmony with the nature.

The difference in Eastern martial arts and general activity lies in the directness of the experience. Direct involvement in the activities and struggles in the process can only enable the practitioners to dig into the unknown self, to enjoy the journey whether it is fully happy or not, to feel the sense of belonging to this universe as part and as a whole, to transcend the pettiness of self, and finally to discover the path to the complete understanding of the bigger self which enables the self to be free to be the best as he/she can be.

In the execution of movement, the mind, technique and breathing must be trinity. The speed varies. Therefore the breathing changes. When the execution and the energy of the breathing become one, there follows a natural speed and power. It is at this point the ki - the energy - spreads all over the body and energizes extraordinary power into the technique. The potential of Taekwondo practitioners are limitless.

# 3 BREATHING AND KI

We cannot survive even a few minutes without breathing. Breathing means living and to live you must breathe. Breathing takes place as inhaling and exhaling and provides necessary oxygen into the body and takes out carbon dioxide from the body.

From breathing starts and ends the Taekwondo training. It is the most fundamental but the most critical in the martial art training. In bending the body occurs exhaling and in erecting, inhaling.

Exhale is the execution of the technique and halt at the moment of impact. Exhaling reduces the internal resistance and maintains the flexibility of the body. In Taekwondo training breathing means the proper use of the ki.

In the Eastern view, breathing has a significant philosophical meaning and the subject belongs to the metaphysical level. In martial art training, breathing equals ki. In Zen training, meditation begins with brathing practice. In Korean terms, there are shimgi, kiryŏk, p'aegi, and hoyŏnjiki. The concept of the ki has been deeply rooted in the daily life of Korean culture.

The oldest legend on the ki is in the record of the book "Samilshingo." It says, "Ki is the power of breathing, the fundamental element to maintain the life form, the potential to create a superhuman power, and the energy for life."

Breathing control in martial art means Tanjŏn Hohŭp (abdomen breathing). What is Tanjŏn? Tanjŏn is located 5-10cm below the belly botton. Tanjŏn Hohŭp stimulates the mental awareness. Tanjŏn actually does not exist, but only illusively. Compared to chest breathing, Tanjŏn Hohŭp does not affect heart beat. It does not give pressure to the heart either. It enhances circulation.

Tanjŏn is an abstract being that is believed to be in the human body, near the center of the body. It is believed to be the source of the energy and activity. The effects of the Tanjŏn breathing are as follows: attainment of mental peace, accumulation of the ki through the enhanced circulation, clear awareness of the mental world through intaking more oxygen.

That is, proper breathing enables you to perform proper techniques, and proper activities bring health. That is why proper basic stances and executions are stressed in the martial art school.

Tanjŏn Hohŭp cosists of inhaling, exhaling, and halting. Halting drives all the energy in the body into the pond of the Tanjŏn, therefore the inner power level increases. When on breathing flows into the parts of the inner body is called Naegi.

The goal of the Tanjŏn breathing is to achieve mental concentration in order to be able to utilize the ki. In training, we hear advice from the instructors, quite often as follows: Don't allow even one opening, get the initiative, or there is an opening. These examples are from the breathing. When there is improper breathing, there is always an opening to attack or to be attacked.

Tanjŏn must be practiced in flexible manner because the location varies according to what type of movement you do. The important factor is to be on harmony with your mind and body, centering your awareness in the Tanjŏn.

Taekwondo is a martial art that uses arm and leg movements in all directions for offense and defense. When the ki is mastered and the Tanjŏn is properly used, each technique will have maximum efficiency. In other words, the mental energy must be transferred to ki through proper breathing.

To have quiet breathing, you must breathe evenly. To have even breathing, you must be aware of the Tanjŏn and breathe deeply. In the performance, totally leave your body to the mind, and let the mind ride on the ki and let the ki explode the techniques, then that is invincible. The trinity of the technique, mind and ki brings perfection.

Every techniques in Taekwondo is designed to develope the ki potential and efficiently utilize proper breathing to bring out the maximum results. Ki is the essence of the Eastern martial art.

# IV

# BASIC MOVEMENTS

# ETIQUETTE AND BASIC MOVEMENT

"Ye" (etiquette) is an essential spirit in Taekwondo training. Taekwondo practice must begin and end with etiquette. Ye is an abbreviation of kyŏngnye. Ye denotes the way that all human beings must follow. It is the fundamental base on which human spirit stands. That is respect for humanity.

Kyŏngnye is a bow that signifies truthful respect to the other person. Kyŏngnye, in Taekwondo practice, is a bow bending the upper body approximately 15 degrees forward. Bowing symbolizes respect without and humility within. Adequate and neat appearance and controlled mental attitude are the most critical in Taekwondo etiquette. Bow is ye and ye can be cultivated through inner effort.

Taekwondo practitioners must bow when entering and leaving the Tojang, when meeting Sabŏmnim, and higher rank students. Before and after working out with partner in self-defense or step-sparring, and performing p'umsae, you must bow in a proper manner.

The goal of Taekwondo training lies in the attainment of the most ideal human values through rigorous physical and mental practice. Where goes the will is where the body follows. The attitude of the mind will eventually determine the way our body will become. With a firm determination of the mind, the body will become strong but flexible enough to meet any challenges of daily life.

Daily practice of appropriate bodily posture and mental carriage are important to bring out successful consequences in Taekwondo training. The basic movements are centra, parts of advanced techniques and any application skills. They require accurate learning and study. Taekwondo utilizes every part of the human body as weapons. Techniques are designed according to kinetic principles. The classifications are punching, thrusting, striking and kicking skills. Stratigical categories are attacking, defending and counter-attacking.

Every technique is based on the proper stance and hand-foot skills. Stance is the first movement for any skills which produce variety of combinations. One basic movement means a combination of stance and kinetic execution of a hand or foot technique.

All basic techniques are supposed to generate a certain amount of force according to the types of technique. To create a maximum power, it is critical to synchronize the three components: smooth execution of technique; mental awareness; and breathing. The equilibrium, adequate shift of center of gravity, concentration are also highly important.

The characteristics of basic movements are determined by the line of the motion such as linear or circular course and the angle of the feet or arms.

Cautions for a good technique :
1. Errect posture and relax the shoulders.
2. Focus the energy at the Tanjŏn.
3. Harmonize the motion and breathing.
4. Keep the balance and shift the body properly.
5. Power must be focused at the final impact.
6. The focus of mind and power must be conscious.

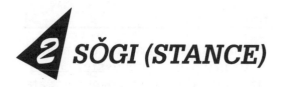

# SŎGI (STANCE)

## CHARYŎT-SŎGI (ATTENTION STANCE)

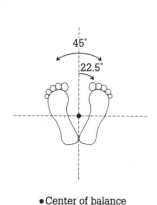

● Center of balance

Feet turned out approximately 45°.
Back straight.
Eyes straight ahead.
Arms at side.

## MOA-SŎGI (CLOSE STANCE)

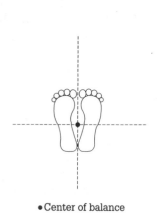

● Center of balance

Close the toes of both feet together.
Back straight. Eyes straight ahead.

# KYŎRUMSE (SPARRING STANCE)

Feet comfortably apart.
Weight evenly distributed for easy maneuvering.
Hands up, elbows in to protect face and upper body.
Head up, eyes on opponent.
Knees bent.
Relax.

# NARANHI-SŎGI (PARALLEL STANCE)

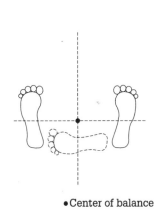

• Center of balance

Feet 1 shoulder width apart.
Both knees straight.
Maintain both feet parallel.

## APKUBI (FORWARD STANCE)

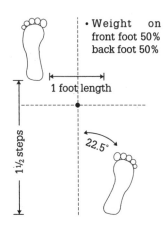

- Weight on front foot 50% back foot 50%

1 foot length

1½ steps

22.5°

Front foot straight ahead.
Front knee over front foot.
Back leg straight with heel on floor.
Back foot angled 22.5°.

Feet approximately 1½ shoulder widths apart front to rear.
This stance is the most stable posture of all.

# APSŎGI (FRONT STANCE)

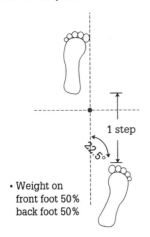

1 step

22.5°

• Weight on
front foot 50%
back foot 50%

Legs almost straight.
Feet approximately shoulder width apart front to rear.
This stance is like the state of standstill in the middle
of walking.

# TWITKUBI (BACKWARD STANCE)

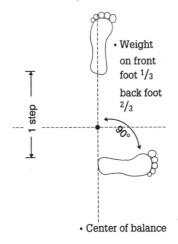

• Weight
on front
foot $1/3$

back foot
$2/3$

1 step

90°

• Center of balance

Feet at 90° angle.
Feet about shoulder width apart.
Both legs slightly bent.
Put 70% of weight or more on back foot.

# PŎM-SŎGI (TIGER STANCE)

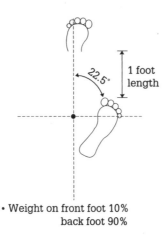

22.5°

1 foot length

• Weight on front foot 10%
back foot 90%

Lift the heel of front foot.
Bend knee of the back leg.
Close both knees to ward each other.
Body weight entirely on the back foot.

# KKOA-SŎGI (CROSS STANCE)

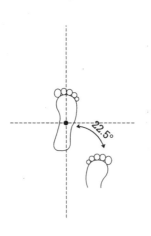

22.5°

Cross both legs.
Lift the heel of back foot.
Press both knees upon each other.

# HAKDARI-SŎGI (CRANE STANCE)

Lift one foot and put it lightly upon the inside of the other knee.
Maintain balance.

# CHUNBI-SŎGI (READY STANCE)

Feet shoulder width apart.
Arms straight.
Make fists.

Eyes straight ahead.

## CHUCH'UM-SŎGI (RIDING STANCE)

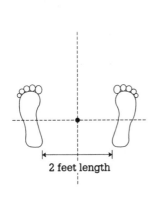

2 feet length

Starting from ch'aryŏt-sŏgi.
Feet 1½ shoulder widths or more apart.
The body weight is balanced equally on two feet.

Back straight.
Bend both knees slightly.

# 3 MAKKI (BLOCK)

## ARAE-MAKKI (LOW BLOCK)

Twisting the wrist, defend low by moving the wrist downward.

When the defense is completed, the body is turned 45° sideways.

The elbow should go no further than the side of the body.

The distance between the wrist and the belly is about two fists.

# ŎLGUL MAKKI (FACE BLOCK)

Defending upward with the outer wrist, with the hand clenched, is the basic form.

# SONNAL-MOMT'ONG-MAKKI (HAND-KNIFE TRUNK BLOCK)

Swing both hand-knifes from over the opposite shoulder.
Block the attack at the height of the face.
Fix the other hand before the stomach.

## MOMT'ONG-AN-MAKKI (TRUNK INSIDE BLOCK)

Block the attack from outside toward inside.
Mostly used on Twitkubi and Apsŏgi.
Fix elbow at the height of stomach.

## MOMT'ONG-PAKKAT-MAKKI (TRUNK OUTSIDE BLOCK)

Block the attack from inside toward outside.
Mostly used on Twitkubi and Apsŏgi.
Fix elbow before the stomach.

# 4 CH'AGI (KICK)

## APCH'AGI (FRONT KICK)

Kicking position.
Bring kicking leg knee up.

Snap leg out to front kick strike with heel with the
toes curled upward.
Snap leg back to complete kick.

## TOLLYŎCH'AGI (TURN KICK)

Kicking position
Cock the kicking leg and start the hips rotating.
Kick, extend kicking leg in an area to attack target.

Follow through with hips, strike with ball or foot of instep.
Snap leg back to complete kick.

# YŎPCH'AGI (SIDE KICK)

Kicking Position.
Back foot is raised to the cocked position ready to kick.

Kick, extend kicking leg and hip, heel up, foot angled down 30°.
Kick with outer edge of foot.
Snap leg back to complete kick.

## TWITCH'AGI (BACK KICK)

Kicking position.
Turn front foot, upper body and head 180°/135° in direction of kicking (rear) leg, as you cock the rear leg to kick.

Kick, spot the target and snap out the kick.
Complete kick by snapping leg back.
Maintain balance, extend hips with kick.
Strike with bottom of heel.

# TWIHURYŎ-CH'AGI (BACK HOOK KICK)

Kicking position.
Turn front foot, upper body and head 180° in direction of kicking (rear) leg, as you cock the rear leg to kick.

Kick, snap the rear leg out and around the opponent's guard to complete the kick.
Strike with heel.

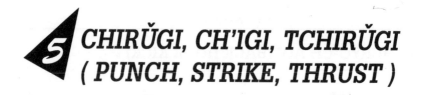

# CHIRŬGI, CH'IGI, TCHIRŬGI ( PUNCH, STRIKE, THRUST )

## MOMT'ONG-CHIRŬGI/CHUCH'UM-SŎGI

Back straight, bend knees slightly.
Set up shins at right angles to the floor tightening inward, and tense on the abdomen.
This stance provides a firm foundation and allows concentration on developing power and form in punching

71 page. The left picture and explanations of Momt'ong-Paro-Chirŭgi should be replaced with the left picture and explanations of Momt'ong-Pandae-Chirŭgi.

# MOMT'ONG-PARO-CHIRŬGI (TRUNK STRAIGHT PUNCH)

The sides of both the leg which is stepped forward and the punching arm are same.

Turn fist to make palmside face downward.

Target the pit of the stomach of the opponent.

# MOMT'ONG-PANDAE-CHIRŬGI (TRUNK REVERSE PUNCH)

The side of the leg which is stepped forward is the opposite of that of the punching arm.

To increase the impact of the trunk punch, use the centrifugal force of the rotating motion of the punching arm and the pulling arm round the waist.

## SONNAL-CH'IGI (HAND-KNIFE STRIKE)

 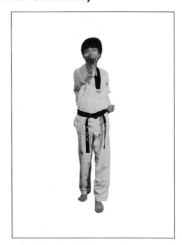

Execute a hand-knife neck strike on Apsŏgi.
Fix both feet and twist the waist slightly.

## SONKKŬT-TCHIRŬGI (SPEARHAND THRUST)

Thrusting surface is tips of fingers.
Finger must be very tense and rigid.
Mostly used on Apkubi.

# V

# P'UMSAE

# T'AEGŬK 1 CHANG

| Number of P'um | Movement (Body and Foot Technique) | Sŏgi | Hand Technique |
|---|---|---|---|
| Chunbi | With the right foot fixed, move the left foot to the left and the F direction. | Naranhi -sŏgi | Kibon-chunbi |
| 1 | Using the right foot, as the axis turn the body to the left while moving the left foot to the L₁ direction. | Oen-apsŏgi | Oen-p'almok-momt'ong-arae-makki |
| 2 | With the left foot fixed, move the right foot one step forward. | Orŭn-apsŏgi | Orŭn-chumŏk-momt'ong-pandae-chirŭgi |
| 3 | Using the left foot as the axis, turn the body to the right while moving the right foot to the R₁ direction. | Orŭn-apsŏgi | Orŭn-p'almok-arae-makki |
| 4 | With the right foot fixed, move the left foot one step forward. | Oen-apsŏgi | Oen-chumŏk-momt'ong-pandae-chirŭgi |
| 5 | Using the right foot as the axis, turn the body to the left while moving the left foot to the F direction. | Oen-apkubi | Oen-p'almok-arae-makki |
| 6 | Keep both feet fixed. | Oen-apkubi | Orŭn-chumŏk-momt'ong-paro-chirŭgi |
| 7 | Using the left foot as the axis, turn the body to the right, moving the right foot to the L₂ direction. | Orŭn-apsŏgi | Oen-pakkat-p'almok-momt'ong-anmakki |
| 8 | With the right foot one step forward. | Oen-apsŏgi | Orŭn-chumŏk-momt'ong-paro-chirŭgi |
| 9 | Using the right foot as the axis, turn the body left while moving the left foot to the L₂ | Oen-apsŏgi | Orŭn-pakkat-p'almok-momt'ong-anmakki |

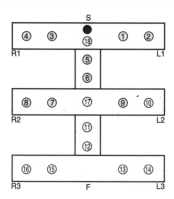

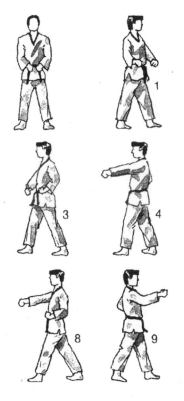

| | | | |
|---|---|---|---|
| | direction. | | |
| 10 | With the left foot fixed, move the right foot one step forward. | Orŭn-apsŏgi | Oen-chumŏk-momt'ong-paro-chirŭgi |
| 11 | Using the left foot as the axis, turn the body right while moving the foot to the F direction. | Orŭn-apkubi | Orŭn-p'almok-arae-makki |
| 12 | Keep both feet fixed. | Orŭn-apkubi | Oen-chumŏk-momt'ong-paro-chirŭgi |
| 13 | Using the right foot as the axis, turn the body left while moving the left foot to the L3 direction. | Oen-apsŏgi | Oen-p'almok-ŏlgul-makki |
| 14 | With the left foot fixed, execute the Apch'agi so that the right foot lands to the front. | Orŭn-apsŏgi | Orŭn-chumŏk-momt'ong-pandae-chirŭgi |
| 15 | Using the left foot as the axis, turn the body right while moving the right foot to the R3 direction. | Orŭn-apsŏgi | Orŭn-p'almok-ŏl-gul-makki |
| 16 | With the right foot fixed, execute the Apch'agi and the left foot lands to the front. | Oen-apsŏgi | Oen-chumŏk-momt'ong-pandae-chirŭgi |
| 17 | Using the right foot as the axis, turn the body to the right while moving the left foot to the S direction. | Oen-apkubi | Oen-p'almok-arae-makki |
| 18 | With the left foot fixed, move the right foot one step forward. | Orŭn-apkubi | Orŭn-chumŏk-momt'ong-pandae-chirŭgi |
| Kŭman | Using the right foot as the axis, turn the body to the left. Move the left foot to the F direction. | Naranhi-sŏgi | Kibon-chunbi |

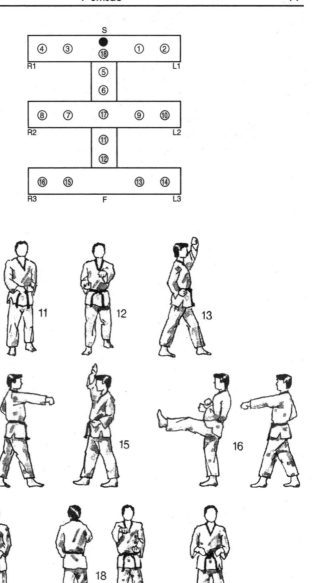

# 2 T'AEGŬK 2 CHANG

| Number of P'um | Movement (Body and Foot Technique) | Sŏgi | Hand Technigue |
|---|---|---|---|
| Chunbi | With the right foot fixed, move the left foot to the left and face the F direction. | Naranhi -Sŏgi | Kibon-chunbi |
| 1 | Using the right foot as the axis, turn the body to the left while moving the left foot to the L₁ direction. | Oen-apsŏgi | Oen-p'almok-arae-makki |
| 2 | With the left foot fixed, move the right foot one step forward. | Oen-apkubi | Orŭn-chumŏk-momt'ong-pandae-chirŭgi |
| 3 | Using the left foot as the axis, turn the body to the right while moving the right foot to the R₁ direction. | Orŭn-apsŏgi | Orŭn-p'almok-arae-makki |
| 4 | With the right foot fixed, move the left foot one step forward. | Oen-apkubi | Oen-chumŏk-momt'ong-pandae-chirŭgi |
| 5 | Using the right foot as the axis, turn the body to the left while moving the left foot to the F direction. | Oen-apsŏgi | Orŭn-pakkat-p'almok-momt'ong-anmakki |
| 6 | With the left foot fixed, move the right foot one step forward. | Orŭn-apsŏgi | Oen-pakkat-p'almok-momt'ong-anmakki |
| 7 | Using the right foot as the axis, turn the body to the left while moving the left foot to the L₂ direction. | Oen-apsŏgi | Oen-p'almok-arae-makki |
| 8 | With the left foot fixed, execute the right Apch'agi so that the right foot lands to the front. | Orŭn-apkubi | Orŭn-chumŏk-ŏl-gul-pandae-chirŭgi |
| 9 | Using the left foot as the axis, turn the body to the right | Orŭn-apsŏgi | Orŭn-p'almok-arae-makki |

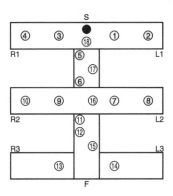

| | | | |
|---|---|---|---|
| | while moving the right foot to the R₂ direction. | | |
| 10 | With the right foot fixed, execute the Apch'agi so that the left foot lands to the front. | Oen-apkubi | Oen-chumŏk-ŏlgul-pandae-chirŭgi |
| 11 | Using the right foot as the axis, turn the body to the left while moving the left to the F direction. | Oen-apsŏgi | Oen-p'almok-ŏlgul-makki |
| 12 | With the left foot fixed, move the right foot one step forward. | Orŭn-apsŏgi | Orŭn-p'almok-ŏlgul-makki |
| 13 | Using the right foot as the axis, turn the body to the left while moving the left foot to the R₃ direction. | Oen-apsŏgi | Orŭn-pakkat-p'almok-momt'ong-anmakki |
| 14 | Using the left foot as the axis, turn the body to the right while moving the right foot to the L₃ direction. | Orŭn-apsŏgi | Oen-pakkat-p'almok-momt'ong-anmakki |
| 15 | Using the right foot as the axis, turn the body to the left while moving the left foot to the S direction. | Oen-apsŏgi | Oen-p'almok-arae-makki |
| 16 | With the left foot fixed, execute the Apch'agi so that the right foot lands to the front. | Orŭn-apsŏgi | Orŭn-chumŏk-momt'ong-pandae-chirŭgi |
| 17 | With the right foot fixed, execute the Apch'agi so that the left foot lands to the front. | Oen-apsŏgi | Oen-chumŏk-momt'ong-pandae-chirŭgi |
| 18 | With the left foot fixed, execute the Apch'agi so that the right foot lands to the front. | Orŭn-apsŏgi | Orŭn-chumŏk-momt'ong-pandae-chirŭgi |
| Kŭman | Using the right foot as the axis, turn the body to the left. Move the left foot to the F direction. | Naranhi-sŏgi | Kibon-chunbi |

# ❸ T'AEGŬK 3 CHANG

| Number of P'um | Movement (Body and Foot Technique) | Sŏgi | Hand Techniqiue |
|---|---|---|---|
| Chunbi | With the right foot fixed, move the left foot to the left and face the F direction. | Naranhi-sŏgi | Kibon-chunbi |
| 1 | Using the right foot as the axis, turn the body to the left while moving the left foot to the $L_1$ direction. | Oen-apsŏgi | Oen-p'almok-arae-makki |
| 2 | With the left foot fixed, execute the Apch'agi so that the right foot lands to the front. | Orŭn-apkubi | Momt'ong-tubŏn-chirŭgi |
| 3 | Using the left foot as the axis, turn the body to the right while moving the right foot to the $R_1$ direction. | Orŭn-apsŏgi | Orŭn-p'almok-arae-makki |
| 4 | With the right foot fixed, execute the Apch'agi so the the left foot lands to the front. | Oen-apkubi | Momt'ong-tubŏn-chirŭgi |
| 5 | Using the right foot as the axis, turn the body to the left while moving the left foot to the F direction. | Oen-apsŏgi | Orŭn-sonnal-mok-ch'igi |
| 6 | With the left foot fixed, move the right foot one step forward. | Orŭn-apsŏgi | Oen-sonnal-mok-ch'igi |
| 7 | With the right foot fixed, move the left foot to the $L_2$ direction. | Orŭn-twitku-bi | Oen-hansonnal-momt'ong-pakkat-makki |
| 8 | Keep the right foot fixed, move the left foot to the $L_2$ direction. | Oen-apkubi | Orŭn-chumŏk-momt'ong-paro-chirŭgi |
| 9 | Using the left foot as the axis, turn the body to the right and face the direction of $R_2$ while moving the right foot slightly | Oen-twitku-bi | Orŭn-hansonnal-momt'ong-pakkat-makki |

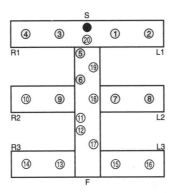

| | | | |
|---|---|---|---|
| | rearward. | | |
| 10 | With the left foot fixed, turn the body right while moving the right foot one step forward. | Orŭn-apkubi | Oen-chumŏk-momt'ong-paro-chirŭgi |
| 11 | Using the right foot as the axis, turn the body to the left while moving the left foot to the F direction. | Oen-apsŏgi | Orŭn-pakkat-p'almok-momt'ong-anmakki |
| 12 | Keeping the left foot fixed, move the right foot one step forward. | Oen-apsŏgi | Oen-pakkat-p'almok-momt'ong-anmakki |
| 13 | Using the right foot as the axis, turn the body to the left while moving the left foot to the R₃ direction. | Oen-apsŏgi | One-p'almok-arae-makki |
| 14 | With the left foot fixed, execute the Apch'agi so that the right foot lands to the front. | Orŭn-apkubi | Momt'ong-tubŏn-chirŭgi |
| 15 | Using the left foot as the axis, turn the body to the right while moving the right foot to the L₃ direction. | Orŭn-apsŏgi | Orŭn-p'almok-arae-makki |
| 16 | With right foot fixed, execute the Apch'agi so that the left foot lands to the front. | Oen-apkubi | Momt'ong-tubŏn-chirŭgi |
| 17 | Using the right foot as the axis, turn the body to the left while moving the left foot to the S direction. | Oen-apsŏgi | Oen-p'almok-arae-makki, Orŭn-chumŏk-momt'ong-paro-chirŭgi |
| 18 | With the left foot fixed, move the right foot one step forward. | Orŭn-apsŏgi | Orŭn-p'almok-arae-makki, Oen-chumŏk-momt'ong-paro-chirŭgi |
| 19 | With the right foot fixed, execute the Apch'agi so that the left foot lands to the front. | Orŭn-apsŏgi | Oen-p'almok-arae-makki, Orŭn-chumŏk-momt'ong-paro- |

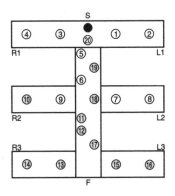

| | | | chirŭgi |
|---|---|---|---|
| 20 | With the left foot fixed, execute the Apch'agi so that the right foot lands to the front. | Oen-apsŏgi | Orŭn-p'almok-arae-makki, Oen-chumŏk-momt'ong-paro-chirŭgi |
| Kŭman | Using the right foot as the axis, turn the body to the left. Move the left foot to the F direction | Naranhi -sŏgi | Kibon-chunbi |

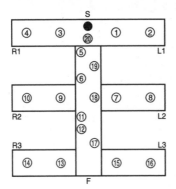

# T'AEGŬK 4 CHANG

| Number of P'um | Movement (Body and Foot Technique) | Sŏgi | Hand Technique |
|---|---|---|---|
| Chunbi | With the right foot fixed, move the left foot to the left and face the F direction. | Naranhi -sŏgi | Kibon-chunbi |
| 1 | With the right foot fixed, turn the body to the L₁ direction while moving the left foot to the L₁ direction. | Orŭn-twitku-bi | Sonnal-momt'ong-makki |
| 2 | With the left foot fixed, move the right foot one step forward. | Orŭn-apkubi | Orŭn-sonkkŭt-sewo tchirŭgi |
| 3 | Using the left foot as the axis, turn the body to the right while moving the right foot to the R₁ direction. | Oen-twitku-bi | Sonnal-momt'ong-makki |
| 4 | With the right foot fixed, move the left foot one step forward. | Oen-apkubi | Oen-sonkkŭt sewo-tchirŭgi |
| 5 | Using the right foot as the axis, turn the body to the left while moving the left foot to the F direction. | Oen-apkubi | Chebip'um-mokch'igi |
| 6 | With the left foot fixed, execute the Apch'agi so that the right foot lands to the front. | Orŭn-apkubi | Oen-chumŏk-momt'ong-paro-chirŭgi |
| 7 | Using the right foot as the axis, execute the Yŏpch'agi to the F direction. | | |
| 8 | Using the left foot as the axis, execute the Yŏpch'agi so that the right foot lands to the front. | Oen-twitku-bi | Sonnal-momt'ong-makki |
| 9 | Using the right foot as the axis, turn the body to the left while moving the left foot to the R₃ direction. | Orŭn-twitku-bi | Momt'ong-pakkat-makki |

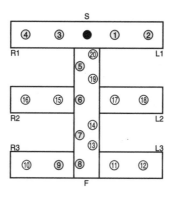

| | | | |
|---|---|---|---|
| 10 | Exeute the Apch'agi with right foot.<br>Move the right foot one step rearward while moving the left foot slightly rearward. | Orŭn-twitku-bi | Momt'ong-anmakki |
| 11 | Using the left foot as the axis, turn the body to the right while moving the right foot to the L₃ direction. | Oen-twitku-bi | Momt'ongpakkat-makki |
| 12 | Execute the Apch'agi with left foot.<br>Move the left foot one step rearward while moving the right foot slightly rearward. | Oen-twitku-bi | Momt'ong-anmakki |
| 13 | Using the right foot as the axis, turn the body to the left while moving the left foot to the S direction. | Oen-apkubi | Chebip'um-mokch'igi |
| 14 | With the left foot fixed, execute Apch'agi so that the right foot lands to the front. | Orŭn-apkubi | Orŭn-dŭngchumŏk-ŏlgul-apch'igi |
| 15 | Using the right foot as the axis, turn the body to the left while moving the left foot to the R₂ direction. | Oen-apsŏgi | Momt'ong-makki |
| 16 | Keep both feet fixed. | Oen-apsŏgi | Momt'ong-paro chirŭgi |
| 17 | Using the left foot as the axis, turn the body the right while moving the right foot to the L₂ direction. | Orŭn-apsŏgi | Momt'ong-makki |
| 18 | Keep both feet fixed. | Orŭn-apsŏgi | Momt'ong-paro chirŭgi |
| 19 | Using the right foot as the axis, turn the body to the left while moving the left foot to the S direction. | Oen-apkubi | Momt'ong-makki,<br>Momt'ong-tubŏn chirŭgi |

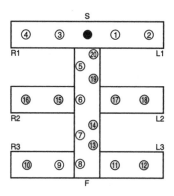

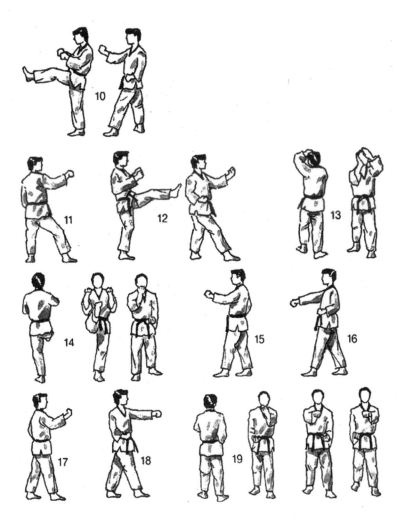

| 20 | With the left foot fixed, move the right foot one step forward. | Orŭn-apkubi | Momt'ong-makki, Momt'ong-tubŏn chirŭgi |
| Kŭman | Using the right foot as the axis, turn the body to the left, Move the left foot to the F direction. | Naranhi -sŏgi | Kibon-chunbi |

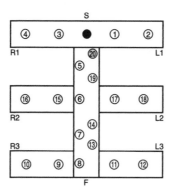

20

# 5 T'AEGŬK 5 CHANG

| Number of P'um | Movement (Body and Foot Technique) | Sŏgi | Hand Technique |
|---|---|---|---|
| Chunbi | With the right foot fixed, move the left foot to the left and face the F direction. | Naranhi-sŏgi | Kibon-chunbi |
| 1 | Using the right foot as the axis, turn the body to the left while moving the left foot to the L₁ direction. | Oen-apkubi | Arae-makki |
| 2 | With the right foot fixed, the left foot is moved rearward, the left hand is moved in a circular motion while executing the left Hammer Fist downward strike. | Oen-pyŏnhi-sŏgi | Mechumŏk-naeryŏch'igi |
| 3 | Using the left foot as the axis, turn the body to the right while moving the right foot to the R₁ direciton. | Orŭn-apkubi | Arae-makki |
| 4 | With the left foot fixed, the right foot is moved rearward. The right hand is moved in a circular motion while executing the Right Hammer Fist downward strike. | Orŭn-pyŏnhi-sŏgi | Mechumŏk-naeryŏch'igi |
| 5 | With the right foot fixed, move the left foot one step forward (F direction). | Oen-apkubi | Momt'ong-makki, Momt'ong-anmakki |
| 6 | With the left foot fixed, execute Apch'agi so that the right foot lands to the front. | Orŭn-apkubi | Orŭn-dŭngchumŏk-apch'igi, Momt'ong-anmakki |
| 7 | With the right foot fixed, execute Apch'agi so that the left foot lands to the front. | Oen-apkubi | Oen-dŭngchumŏk-ŏlgul-apch'igi, Momt'ong-anmakki |
| 8 | With the left foot fixed, move | Orŭn- | Orŭn-deungjumŏk- |

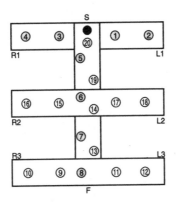

| | | | |
|---|---|---|---|
| | the right foot one step forward. | apkubi | ŏlgul-apch'igi |
| 9 | Using the right foot as the axis, turn the body to the left while moving the left foot to the R₃ direction. | Orŭn-twitku-bi | Oen-hansonnal-momt'ong-yŏpmakki |
| 10 | With the left foot fixed, move the right foot one step forward R₃ direction. | Orŭn-apkubi | Orŭn-p'algup-momt'ong-ch'igi |
| 11 | Using the left foot as the axis, turn the body to the right while moving the right foot to the L₃ direction. | Oen-twitku-bi | Orŭn-hansonnal-momt'ong-yŏpmakki |
| 12 | With the right foot fixed, move the left foot one step forward L₃ direction. | Oen-apkubi | Oen-p'algup-momt'ong-ch'igi |
| 13 | Using the right foot as the axis, turn the body to the left while moving the left foot to the S direction. | Oen-apkubi | Arae-makki ⇒ Momt'ong-anmakki |
| 14 | With the left foot fixed, execute the Apch'agi so that the right foot lands to the front S. | Orŭn-Apkubi | Arae-makki ⇒ Momt'ong-anmakki |
| 15 | Using the right foot as the axis, turn the body to the left while moving the left foot to the R₂ direciton. | Oen-Apkubi | Ŏlgul-makki |
| 16 | With the left foot fixed, execute the Yŏpch'agi so that the right foot lands to the front R₂ direction. | Orŭn-apkubi | Oen-p'algup-momt'ong-pyojŏk-ch'igi |
| 17 | Using the left foot as the axis, turn the body to the right while moving the right foot to the L₂ direction. | Orŭn-apkubi | Ŏlgul-makki |
| 18 | With the right foot fixed, execute the Yŏpch'agi so that the left foot lands to the front L₂ direction. | Oen-apkubi | Orŭn-p'algup-momt'ong-p'yojŏk-ch'igi |
| 19 | Using the right foot as the axis, turn the body to the left | Oen-apkubi | Arae-makki ⇒ Momt'ong- |

| | | | |
|---|---|---|---|
| | while moving the left foot to the S direction. | | anmakki |
| 20 | Execute the Apch'agi so that both feet spring forward and the right foot lands to the front. The left foot should land directly behind the right foot. | Orŭn-kkoa-sŏgi | Orŭn-dŭngchumŏk-ŏlgul-apch'igi (swiftly)>Kihap< |
| Kŭman | Using the right foot as the axis, turn the body to the left and face the F direction. | Naranhi-sŏgi | Kibon-chunbi |

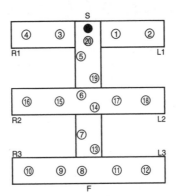

20

# 6 T'AEGŬK 6 CHANG

| Number of P'um | Movement (Body and Foot Technique) | Sŏgi | Hand Technique |
|---|---|---|---|
| Chunbi | With the right foot fixed, move the left foot to the left and face the F direction . | Naranhi -sŏgi | Kibon-chunbi |
| 1 | Using the right foot as the axis, turn the body to the left while moving the left foot to the $L_1$ direction. | Oen-apkubi | Arae-makki |
| 2 | Execute the Apch'agi with the right foot. Return the right foot to its original position and assume Twitkubi. | Orŭn-twitku-bi | Momt'ong-pakkat-makki |
| 3 | Using the left foot as the axis, turn the body to the right while moving the right foot to the $R_1$ direction. | Orŭn-apkubi | Arae-makki |
| 4 | Execute the Apch'agi with the left foot. Return the left foot to its original position and assume Twitkubi. | Oen-twitku-bi | Momt'ong-pakkat-makki |
| 5 | Using the left foot as the axis, turn the body to the left while moving the right foot to the F direction. | Oen-apkubi | Orŭn-hansonnal-ŏl-gul-pakkat-makki |
| 6 | Using the right foot as the axis, execute the Tollyŏch'agi with the right foot. The right foot lands to the front. Move the left foot to the $L_2$ direction. | Oen-apkubi | Ŏlgul-pakkat-makki and then swiftly Momt'ong-paro-chirŭgi |
| 7 | With the left foot fixed, execute the Apch'agi with right foot so that the right foot lands to the front $L_2$ direction. | Orŭn-apkubi | Momt'ong-paro-chirŭgi (swiftly) |
| 8 | Using the left foot as the axis, | Orŭn- | Ŏlgul-pakkat-mak- |

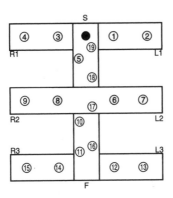

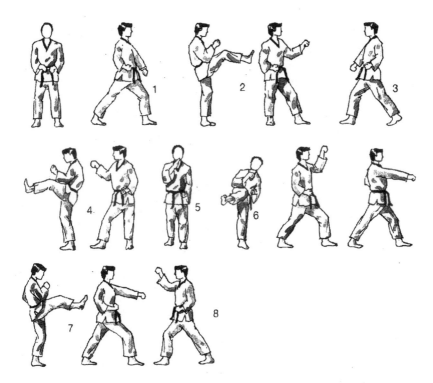

| | | | |
|---|---|---|---|
| | turn the body to the right while moving the right foot to the R₂ direction. | apkubi | ki and then swiftly Momt'ong-paro-chirŭgi |
| 9 | With the right foot fixed, execute the Apch'agi with the left foot so that the left foot lands to the front. | Oen-apkubi | Momtong-baro-chireugi (swiftly) |
| 10 | Using the right foot as the axis, turn the body to the left while moving the left foot to the L₂ direction. | Naranhi-sŏgi | Arae-hech'yŏ-makki (slowly) |
| 11 | With the left foot fixed, move the right foot one step forward F direction. | Orŭn-apkubi | Oen-hansonnal-ŏl-gul-pakkat-makki |
| 12 | With the right foot fixed, execute Tollyŏc-h'agi with the left foot.>Kihap< The left foot lands to the front (F direction). Turn the body to the right and move the right foot to the L₃ direction. | Orŭn-apkubi | Arae-makki (swiftly) |
| 13 | Execute the Apch'agi with the left foot. Return the left foot to its original position and assume Twitkubi. | Oen-twitku-bi | Momt'ong-pakkat-makki |
| 14 | Using the right foot as the axis, turn the body to the left while moving the left foot to the R₃ direction. | Oen-apkubi | Arae-makki (swiftly) |
| 15 | Execute Apch'agi with the right foot. Assume the Twitkubi. | Orŭn-twitku-bi | Momt'ong-pakkat-makki |
| 16 | Using the left foot as the axis, turn the body to the right while moving the right foot to the S direction. | Orŭn-twitku-bi | Sonnal-momt'ong-makki |
| 17 | Using the right foot as the axis, turn the body to the left while moving the left foot to the S direction. | Oen-twitku-bi | Sonnal-momt'ong-makki |
| 18 | Using the left foot as the axis, | Oen- | Pat'angson- |

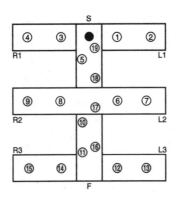

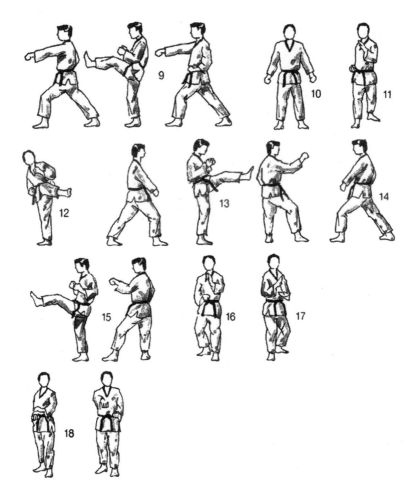

| | | | |
|---|---|---|---|
| | turn the body to the right while moving the left foot to the S direction. | apkubi | momt'ong-makki |
| | Keep both feet fixed. | Orŭn-apkubi | Momt'ong-paro-chirŭgi |
| 19 | With the right foot fixed, move the left foot one step rearward (S direction). | Oen-apkubi | Pat'angson-momt'ong-makki |
| | Keep both feet fixed. | Orŭn-apkubi | Momt'ong-paro-chirŭgi |
| Kŭman | With the left foot fixed, move the right foot rearward. | Naranhi-sŏgi | Kibon-chunbi |

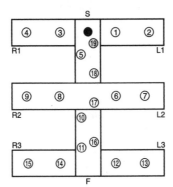

19

| Number of P'um | Movement (Body and Foot Technique) | Sŏgi | Hand Technique |
|---|---|---|---|
| Chunbi | With the right foot fixed, move the left foot to the left and face F direction. | Naranhi-sŏgi | Kibon-chunbi |
| 1 | Using the right foot as the axis, turn the body to the left. | Oen-pŏmsŏgi | Pat'angson-momt'ong-anmakki |
| 2 | With the left foot fixed, execute the Apch'agi with the right foot and returthe right foot to its original position. | Oen-pŏmsŏgi | Momt'ong-makki |
| 3 | Using the left foot as the axis, turn the body to the right (R₁ direction). | Orŭn-pŏmsŏgi | Pat'angson-momt'ong-anmakki |
| 4 | With the right foot fixed, execute the Apch'agi with the left foot and return the left to its original position. | Orŭn-pŏmsŏgi | Momt'ong-makki |
| 5 | With the right foot fixed, move the left foot to the F direction. | Orŭn-twitkubi | Sonnal-arae-makki |
| 6 | With the left foot fixed, move the right foot one step forward (F direction). | Oen-twitkubi | Sonnal-arae-makki |
| 7 | With the right foot fixed, move the left foot to the L₂ direction. | Oen-pŏmsŏgi | Kŏdŭrŏ-pat'angson-anmakki |
| 8 | From the same stance. | Oen-pŏmsŏgi | Orŭn-dŭngchumŏk-apch'igi (swiftly) |
| 9 | With the both feet fixed, turn the body to the right and face R₂ direction. | Orŭn-pŏmsŏgi | Kŏdŭrŏ-pat'angson-anmakki |
| 10 | From the same stance. | Orŭn- | Oen-dŭngchumŏk- |

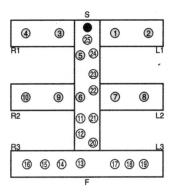

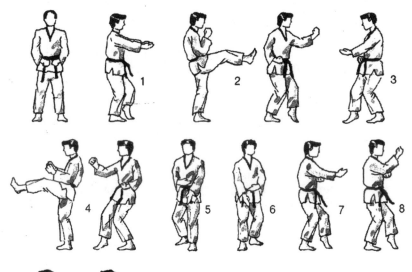

| | | pŏmsŏgi | apchigi |
|---|---|---|---|
| 11 | Using the left foot as the axis, turn the body to the left while moving the right foot beside the left foot (F direction). | Moasŏgi | Pojumŏk |
| 12 | With the right foot fixed, move the left foot one step forward. | Oenapkubi | Tubŏn-kawi-makki<br>1. Orŭn-p'almok-arae-makki and Oen-p'almok-momt'ong-makki<br>2. Oen-p'almok-arae-makki and Orŭn-p'almok-momt'ong-makki |
| 13 | With the left foot fixed, move the right foot one step forward. | Orŭnapkubi | Tubŏn-kawi-makki |
| 14 | Using the right foot as the axis, turn the body to the left while moving the left foot to the R₃ direction. | Oenapkubi | Pakkat-p'almok-momt'ong-hech'yŏ-makki |
| 15 | Execute the Murŭp-ch'igi. Keep the right leg cocked, having both fists to the sides. | Orŭnkkoasŏgi | Tuchumŏk-momt'ong-chech'yŏ-chirŭgi |
| 16 | Keep the right foot fixed, move the left foot one step rearward. | Orŭnapkubi | Ŏtgŏrŏ-arae-makki |
| 17 | Using the left foot as the axis, turn the body to the right while moving the right foot to the L₃ direction. | Orŭnapkubi | Pakkat-p'almok-momt'ong-hech'yŏ-makki |
| 18 | Execute the Murŭp-ch'igi. Keep the left foot cocked, having bothe fists to the sides. | Oenkkoasŏgi | Tuchumŏk-momt'ong chech'yo-chirŭgi |
| 19 | Keep the left foot fixed, move the right foot one step rearward. | Oenapkubi | Ŏtgŏrŏ-arae-makki |
| 20 | Using the right foot as the axis, turn the body to the left and | Oenapsŏgi | Oen-dŭngchumŏk-ŏlgul-pakkat-ch'igi |

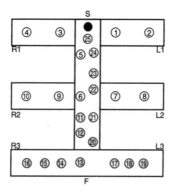

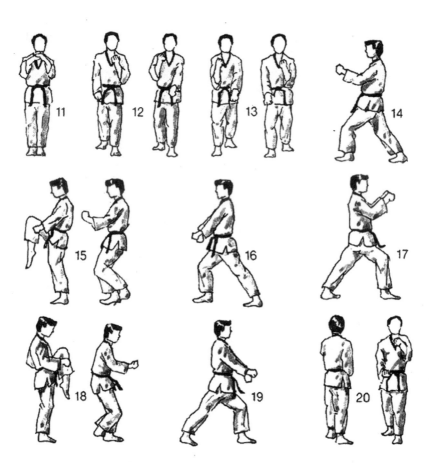

| | | | (swiftly) |
|---|---|---|---|
| | move the left foot to the S direction. | | |
| 21 | Execute the Pyojŏk-ch'agi (S direction). | Chuch'-um-sŏgi | Orŭn-p'algup-p'yojŏk-ch'igi |
| 22 | Keeping the right foot fixed, move the left foot slightly forward (S direction). | Orŭn-apsŏgi | Orŭn-dŭngchumŏk-ŏlgul-pakkat-ch'igi (swiftly) |
| 23 | Execute the Pyojŏk-chagi (S direction). | Chuch'-um-sŏgi | Oen-p'algup-p'yojŏk-ch'igi |
| 24 | Keep both feet fixed. | Chuch'-um-sŏgi | Oen-hansonnal-momt'ong-yŏpmak-ki |
| 25 | With the left foot fixed. Move the right foot to the S direction. | Chuch'-um-sŏgi | Orŭn-yŏp-chirŭgi (Place the left hand to the left side.) >Kihap< |
| Kŭman | Using the right foot as the axis, turn the body to the left. | Naranhi-sŏgi | Kibon-chunbi |

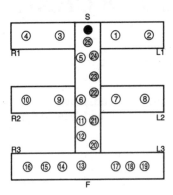

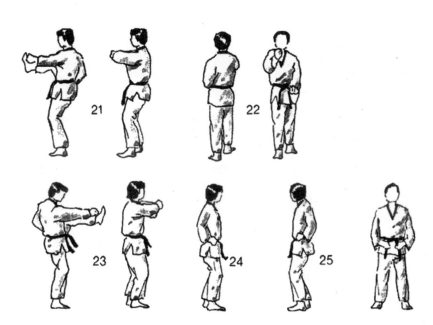

# 8 T'AEGǓK 8 CHANG

| Number of P'um | Movement (Body and Foot Technique) | Sǒgi | Hand Technique |
|---|---|---|---|
| Chunbi | With the right foot fixed, move the left foot to the left and face F direction. | Naranhi-sǒgi | Kibon-chunbi |
| 1 | With the right foot fixed, move the left foot one step forward (F direction). | Orǔn-twitku-bi (then swiftly) | Pakkat-p'almok-momt'ong-kǒdǔrǒ-makki |
| 2 | | Oen-apkubi | Momt'ong-paro-chirǔgi |
| 3 | Execute the Tubal-dangsǒng-apch'agi. >Kihap<. The feet land to the front (F direction). | Oen-apkubi | Momt'ong-makki ⇨ Momt'ong-tubǒn chirǔgi |
| 4 | With the left foot fixed, move the right foot one step forward. | Orǔn-apkubi | Momt'ong-pandae-chirǔgi |
| 5 | Using the right foot as the axis, turn the body to the left while moving the left foot to the R₃ direction. | Orǔn-apkubi | Oesantǔl-makki |
| 6 | Turn the body to the left (R₃ direction). | Oen-apkubi | Orǔn-chumǒk-tanggyǒ-t'ǒkch'igi |
| 7 | Bring the left foot over the right L₃ direction and assume the Kkoa-sǒgi then move the right foot to the L₃ direction. | Oen-apkubi | Oesantǔl-makki |
| 8 | Turn the body to the right without the feet. | Orǔn-apkubi | Oen-chumǒk-tang-gyǒ-t'ǒkch'igi |
| 9 | Using the left foot as the axis, turn the body to the left while moving the right foot to the S direction. | Orǔn-twitku-bi | Sonnal-momt'ong-makki |
| 10 | With the right foot fixed, move the left foot slightly forward (F | Oen-apkubi | Momt'ong-paro-chirǔgi |

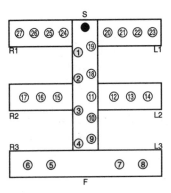

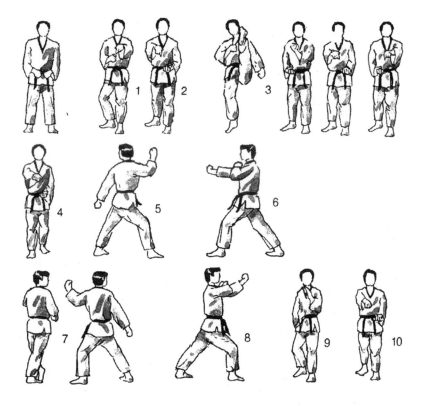

| | | | |
|---|---|---|---|
| | direction). | | |
| 11 | Execute the Apch'agi with right foot and bring the right foot back to its original position then move the left foot one step rearward. | Orŭn-pŏmsŏ-gi | Pat'angson-momt'ong-makki |
| 12 | With the right foot fixed, move the left foot to the L₂ direction. | Oen-pŏmsŏ-gi | Sonnal-momt'ong-makki |
| 13 | With the right foot fixed, execute the Apch'agi with left foot so that the left foot lands to the front (L₂ direction). | Oen-apkubi | Momt'ong-paro-chirŭgi (swiftly) |
| 14 | With the right foot fixed, move the left foot slightly rearward. | Oen-pŏmsŏ-gi | Pat'angson-momt'ong-makki (swiftly) |
| 15 | Turn the body to the right without moving the feet (R₂ direction). | Orŭn-pŏmsŏ-gi | Sonnal-momt'ong-makki |
| 16 | With the lefe foot fixed, execute the Apch'agi with right foot so that the right foot lands to the front (R₂ direction). | Orŭn-apkubi | Momt'ong-paro-chirŭgi (swiftly) |
| 17 | With the left foot fixed, move the right foot slightly rearward. | Orŭn-pŏmsŏ-gi | Pat'angson-momt'ong makki (swiftly) |
| 18 | Using the left foot as the axis, trun the body to the right while moving the right foot to the S direction. | Oen-twitku-bi | Kŏdŭrŏ-arae-makki |
| 19 | Execute the Apch'agi with left foot ther Apch'agi with right foot in spring. The left foot lands where the right foot was. | Orŭn-apkubi | Momt'ong-makki and then Oen-orŭn-momt'ong chirŭgi (swiftly) |
| 20 | Using the right foot as the axis, turn the body to the left while moving the left foot to the L₁ direction. | Orŭn-twitku-bi | Hansonnal-momt'ong-yŏp-makki |
| 21 | With the right foot fixed, move | Oen- | Orŭn-p'algup-ŏlgul |

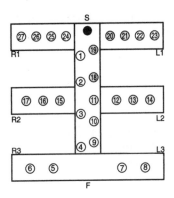

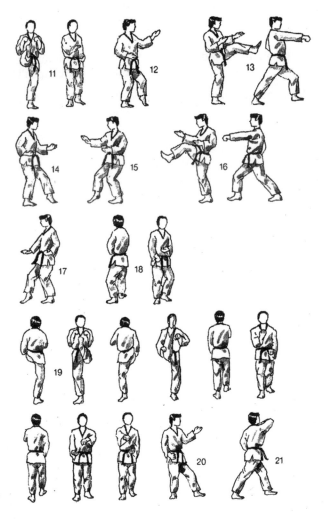

|  | the left foot slightly forward (L₁ direction). | apkubi | -tollyŏch'igi |
|---|---|---|---|
| 22 | With both feet fixed. | Oen-apkubi | Orŭn-dŭngchumŏk-apch'igi |
| 23 | With both feet fixed. | Oen-apkubi | Momt'ong-pandae-chirŭgi |
| 24 | With the left foot fixed, turn the body to the right (R₁ direction) while pulling the right foot slightly backward. | Oen-twitku-bi | Hansonnal-momt'ong-yŏp-makki |
| 25 | With the left foot fixed, move the right foot slightly forward (R₁ direction). | Orŭn-apkubi | Oen-p'algup-ŏlgul-tollyŏ-ch'igi (swiftly) |
| 26 | With both feet fixed. | Orŭn-apkubi | Oen-dŭngchumŏk-ŏlgul-apch'igi |
| 27 | With both feet fixed. | Orŭn-apkubi | Momt'ong-pandae-chirŭgi |
| Kŭman | With the right foot fixed, move the left foot toward the right foot. Turn the body to the left. | Naranhi-sŏgi | Kibon-chunbi |

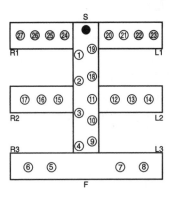

# 9 KORYŎ

| Number of P'um | Movement (Body and Foot Technique) | Sŏgi | Hand Technique |
|---|---|---|---|
| Chunbi | With the right foot fixed, move the left foot to the side. Raise both hands up to face level with the palms. | Naranhi-sŏgi | T'ongmilgi-chunbi |
| 1 | With the right foot fixed, trun the body to the left ($L_1$ direction). | Orŭn-twitku-bi | Sonnal-momt'ong-makki |
| 2 | With the left foot fixed, execute the Arae-yŏpch'agi, followed by the Momt'ong-yŏpch'agi with the same foot so that the right foot lands to the front ($L_1$ direction). | Orŭn-apkubi | Sonnal-pakkat-ch'igi |
| 3 | While keeping both feet fixed. | Orŭn-apkubi | Momt'ong-paro-chirŭgi |
| 4 | With the left foot fixed, move the right foot slightly toward the left. | Oen-twitku-bi | Momt'ong-makki |
| 5 | Using the left foot as the axis, turn the body to the right while moving the right foot to the $R_1$ direction. | Oen-twitku-bi | Sonnal-momt'ong-makki |
| 6 | With the right foot fixed, execute the Arae-yŏpch'agi with left foot, followed by the Momt'ong-yŏpch'agi with the same foot so that the left foot lands to the front ($R_1$ direction). | Oen-apkubi | Sonnal-pakkat-ch'igi |
| 7 | With both feet fixed. | Orŭn-apkubi | Momt'ong-paro-chirŭgi |
| 8 | With the right foot fixed, bring the left foot slightly toward the right foot. | Orŭn-twitku-bi | Momt'ong-makki |
| 9 | Using the right foot as the ax- | Oen- | Oen-hansonnal- |

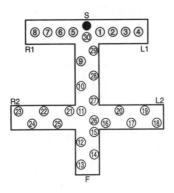

| | | | |
|---|---|---|---|
| | is, turn the body to the left while moving the left foot to the F direction. | apkubi | arae-makki ⇒ Orŭn-k'aljebi |
| 10 | With the left foot fixed, execute the Apch'agi with the right foot so that the right foot lands to the front (F direction). | Orŭn-apkubi | Orŭn-hansonnal arae-makki ⇒ Orŭn-k'aljebi >Kihap< |
| 11 | With the right foot fixed, execute the Apch'agi with the left foot so that the left foot lands to the front (F direction). | Oen-apkubi | Oen-hansonnal-arae-makki ⇒ Orŭn-k'aljebi >Kihap< |
| 12 | With the left foot fixed, execute the Apchagi with the right foot so that the right foot lands to the front (F direction). | Orŭn-apkubi | Murŭp-kkogi |
| 13 | Using the right foot as the axis, turn the body to the right while moving the left foot one step forward. | Orŭn-apkubi | Anp'almok-momt'ong-hech'yŏ-makki |
| 14 | With the right foot fixed, execute the Apch'agi with the left foot so that the left foot lands to the front (S direction). | Oen-apkubi | Murŭp-kkogi |
| 15 | With the right foot fixed, move the left foot slightly rearward. | Oen-apsŏgi | Anp'almok-momt'ong-hech'yŏ-makki |
| 16 | Using the right foot as the axis, turn the body to the right while moving the right foot to the L₂ direction. | Chuch'-um-sŏgi | Oen-hansonnal-y-ŏpmakki |
| 17 | While keeping both feet fixed. | Chuch'-um-sŏgi | Orŭn-chumŏk-pyojŏk-ch'igi |
| 18 | The right foot crosses in front of the left foot to make the kkoa-sŏgi. Bring the fists to the right side. Execute the Yŏpch'agi with the left foot to the L₂ direction so that the left foot lands to | Orŭn-apkubi | Oen-p'yŏnsonkkŭt-chech'yo-tchirŭgi |

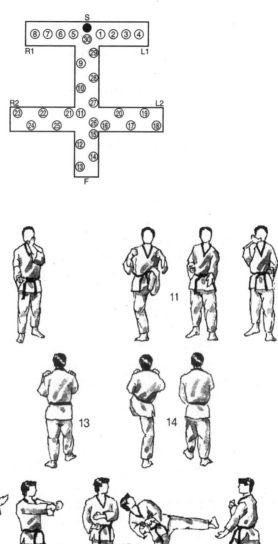

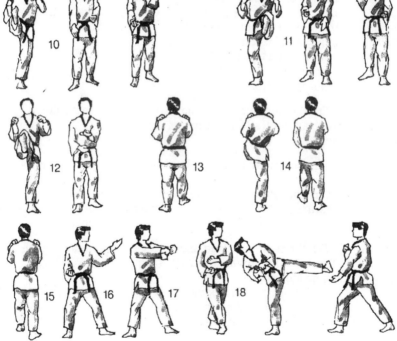

| | | | |
|---|---|---|---|
| | the front. | | |
| 19 | With the left foot fixed, move the right foot slightly toward the rear. | Orŭn-apsŏgi | Arae-makki |
| 20 | Move the left foot one step forward (R₂ direction). | Oen-apsŏgi | Oen-pat'angson-momt'ong-nullŏ-makki |
| 21 | Keeping both feet fixed in the Chuch'um-sŏgi | Chuch'-um-sŏgi | Orŭn-hansonnal-momt'ong-yŏp-makki |
| 22 | Keeping both feet fixed. | Chuch'-um-sŏgi | Oen-chumŏk-p'yojŏk -ch'igi |
| 23 | Cross the left foot over the rioght foot to form the kkoa-sŏgi. Move the fists to the left side, then execute Yŏpch'agi with the right foot to the R₂ direction so that the right foot lands to the front. | Chuch'-um-sŏgi | Orŭn-p'yŏn-sonkkŭt-chech'ŏ-tchirŭgi |
| 24 | With the right foot fixed, move the left foot slightly toward the rear. | Oen-apsŏgi | Arae-makki |
| 25 | More the right foot one step forward. (L₂ direction) More the left foot one step forward. | Chuch'-um-sŏgi Chuch'-um-sŏgi | Orŭn-pat'angson-momt'ong-nullŏ-makki, Oen-p'algup-yŏpch'igi |
| 26 | With the right foot fixed, move the left foot inward and assume Moa-sŏgi. Raise both hands above the head in a circular motion, move them to waist level. | Moa-sŏgi | Oen-hansonnal-p'yojŏk-ch'igi |
| 27 | Using the right foot as the asix,turn the body to the left while moving the left foot to the S direction. | Oen-apkubi | Oen-hansonnal-arae-makki |
| 28 | With the left foot fixed, move the right foot one step forward | Orŭn-apkubi | Orŭn-hansonnal-mokch'igi ⇨ Orŭn- |

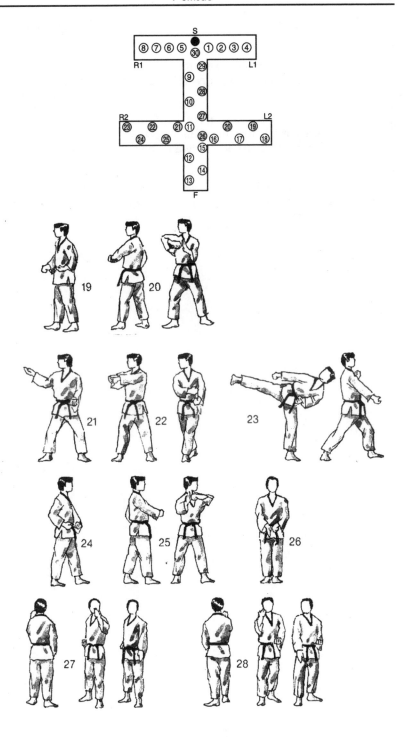

| | (S direction). | | hansonnal-arae-makki |
|---|---|---|---|
| 29 | With the right foot fixed, move the left foot one step forward. | Oen-apkubi | Oen-hansonal-mokchigi ⇒ Oen-hansonnal-arae-makki |
| 30 | With the left foot fixed, move the right foot one step forward (S direction). | Orŭn-apkubi | Orŭn-k'aljebi >Kihap< |
| Kŭman | Using the right foot as the axis, turn the body to the left. | Naranhi-sŏgi | T'ongmilgi-chunbi |

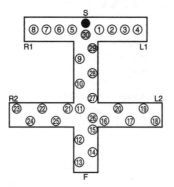

# 10 KŬMGANG

| Number of P'um | Movement (Body and Foot Technique) | Sŏgi | Hand Technique |
|---|---|---|---|
| Chunbi | With the right foot fixed, move the left foot to the left and face the F direction. | Naranhi -sŏgi | Kibon-chunbi |
| 1 | With the right foot fixed, move the left foot one step forward (F direction). | Oen-apkubi | Anp'almok-momt'ong-hech'yŏ-makki |
| 2 | With the left foot fixed, move the right foot one step forward. | Orŭn-apkubi | Orŭn-pat'angson-t'ŏkch'igi |
| 3 | With the right foot fixed, move the left foot one step forward. | Oen-apkubi | Oen-pat'angson-t'ŏkch'igi |
| 4 | With the lefe foot fixed, move the right foot one step forward. | Orŭn-apkubi | Orŭn-pat'angson-t'ŏkch'igi |
| 5 | With the left foot fixed, move the right foot one step to the rear (S direction). | Orŭn-twitkubi | Hansonnal-momt'ong-makki |
| 6 | With the right foot fixed, move the left foot one step to the rear. | Orŭn-twitkubi | Hansonnal-momt'ong-makki |
| 7 | With the left foot fixed, move the right foot one step to the rear. | Oen-twitkubi | Hansonnal-momt'ong-makki |
| 8 | With the right foot fixed, lift the left foot up and assume the Hakdari-sŏgi. Execute the right wrist for the Ŏlgul-makki and the left wrist for the Arae-makki slowly but forcibly. look toward the L direction. | Orŭn-hakdari-sŏgi | Kŭmgang-makki |
| 9 | With the right foot fixed, put the leftfoot on the ground (L direction). | Chuch'-um-sŏgi | Oen-kŭn-toltchŏgwi |

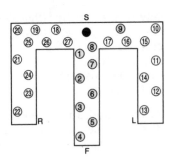

| 10 | Turn the body to the left by pivoting on the ball of the left foot, then step forward with the right foot pivot on the ball of the right foot and move the left foot to the L direction. | Chuch'-um-sŏgi | Oen-kŭn-toltchŏgwi |
|----|----|----|----|
| 11 | With the left foot fixed, turn the body to the left while powerfully returning the right foot to the ground (L direction). | Chuch'-um-sŏgi | Santŭl-makki |
| 12 | Using the right foot as the axis, turn the body to the right while moving the left foot to the L direction. | Chuch'-um-sŏgi | Anp'almok-momt'ong-hech'yŏ-makki |
| 13 | With the right foot fixed, move the left foot rearward. | Chuch'-um-sŏgi | Arae-hech'yŏ-makki (Slowly and forcibly) |
| 14 | Using the right foot as the axis, turn the body to the right while powerfully returning the left foot to the ground (L direction). | Naranhi-sŏgi | Santŭl-makki |
| 15 | Using the left foot as the axis, turn the body to the right while lifting the right foot up and assume Hakdari-sŏgi. Execute the left wrist for the Ŏl-gul-makki and the right wrist for the Arae-makki slowly but forcibly. Look toward the R direction. | Oen-hakdari-sŏgi | Kŭmgang-makki |
| 16 | With the left foot fixed, put the right foot on the ground (R direction). | Chuch'-um-sŏgi | Orŭn-kŭn-toltchŏgwi |
| 17 | Turn the body to the right by pivoting on the ball of the right foot and move the foot to the R direction, then rotate the body 360 and move the right foot to the R direction swiftly. | Chuch'-um-sŏgi | Orŭn-kŭn-toltchŏgwi |
| 18 | With the left foot fixed, move | Oen- | Kŭmgang-makki |

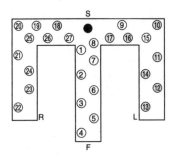

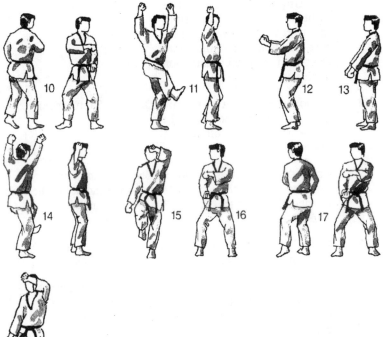

10  11  12  13

14  15  16  17

18

| | | | |
|---|---|---|---|
| | the right foot forward and assume Hakdari-sŏgi with the left foot then execute the left wrist for the Ŏlgul-makki and the right wrist for the Arae-makki. Look toward the R direction. | hakdari-sŏgi | |
| 19 | With the lefe foot fixed, return the right foot to the ground (R direction). | Chuch'-um-sŏgi | Orŭn-kŭn-toltchŏgwi |
| 20 | Turn the body to the right by pivoting on the ball of the right foot and move the right foot to the R direction then rotate the body 360 and move the right foot to the R direction swiftly. | Chuch'-um-sŏgi | Orŭn-kŭn-toltchŏgwi |
| 21 | Using the right foot as the axis, turn the body to the right while moving the left foot to the R direction. | Chuch'-um-sŏgi | Santŭl-makki |
| 22 | Using the left foot as the axis, turn the body to the left while moving the right foot to the F direction. | Chuch'-um-sŏgi | Anp'almok-momt'ong-hech'yo-makki |
| 23 | With the left foot fixed, move the right foot rearward. | Naranhi-sŏgi | Arae-hech'yŏ-makki |
| 24 | Using the left foot as the axis, turn the body to the left while returning the right foot to the ground (R direction). | Chuch'-um-sŏgi | Santŭl-makki |
| 25 | Using the right foot as the axis, turn the body to the left while lifting the left foot up and assume Hakdari-sŏgi with the right foot, then execute the right wrist for the Ŏlgul-makki and the left wrist for the Arae-makki slowly and forcibly. Look toward the R direction. | Orŭn-hakdari-sŏgi | Kŭmgang-makki |

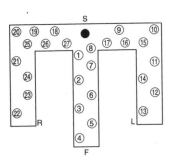

| 26 | With the right foot fixed, retrun the left foot to the ground (L direction). | Chuch'-um-sŏgi | Oen-kŭn-toltchŏgwi |
|---|---|---|---|
| 27 | Turn the body to the left by pivoting on the ball of the left foot and move the left foot to the L direction. Rotate the body 360° and move the left foot to the L direction. | Chuch'-um-sŏgi | Oen-kŭn toltchŏgwi (swiftly) |
| Kŭman | With the right foot fixed, move the left foot toward the right foot. | Naranhi -sŏgi | Kibon-chunbi |

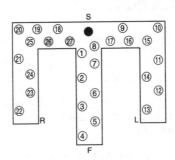

26        27

# 11 TAEBAEK

| Number of P'um | Movement (Body and Foot Technique) | Sŏgi | Hand Technique |
|---|---|---|---|
| Chunbi | With the right foot fixed, move the left foot to the left and face the direction of F. | Naranhi -sŏgi | Kibon-chunbi |
| 1 | Using the right foot as the axis, turn the body to the left while moving the left foot to the L₁ direction. | Oen-pŏmsŏ-gi | Sonnal-arae-hech'yŏ-makki |
| 2 | With the left foot fixed, execute the Apch'agi with the right foot so that the right foot lands to the front. | Orŭn-apkubi | Momt'ong-tubŏn-chirŭgi |
| 3 | Using the left foot as the axis, turn the body to the right while moving the right to the R₁ direction. | Orŭn-pŏmsŏ-gi | Sonnal-arae-hech'yŏ-makki |
| 4 | With the right foot fixed, execute the Apch'agi with the left foot so that the left foot lands to the front (R₁ direction). | Oen-apkubi | Momt'ong-tubŏn-chirŭgi |
| 5 | Using the right foot as the axis, turn the body to the left while moving the left to the F direction. | Oen-apkubi | Chebip'um-mokch'igi |
| 6 | With the left foot fixed, move the right foot one step forward (F direction). | Orŭn-apkubi | Momt'ong-paro-chirŭgi |
| 7 | with the right foot fixed, move the left hand down and out with the palm oriented downward and move the left foot one step forward (F direction). | Oen-apkubi | Momt'ong-paro-chirŭgi |
| 8 | With the left foot fixed, move the right hand down and out in a scooping motion, and | Orŭn-apkubi | Momt'ong-paro-chirŭgi |

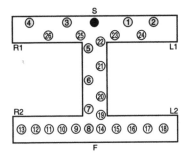

| | | | |
|---|---|---|---|
| | move the right foot one step (F direction). | | |
| 9 | Using the right foot as the axis, turn the body to the left while moving the left foot to the L₂ direction. | Orŭn-twitku-bi | Momt'ong-kŭmgang-makki |
| 10 | While keeping both feet fixed. | Orŭn-twitku-bi | Tanggyŏ-t'ŏkch'igi |
| 11 | While keeping both feet fixed. | Orŭn-twitku-bi | Oen-chumŏk-yŏpchirŭgi |
| 12 | With the right foot fixed, life the left foot up. | Orŭn-hakdari-sŏgi | Orŭn-toltchŏgwi |
| 13 | With the right foot fixed, execute the yŏpch'agi with left foot so that the left foot lands to the front R₂ direction. | Oen-apkubi | Orŭn-p'algup-p'yojŏk-ch'igi |
| 14 | Move the left foot foward the right foot and assume the Moa-sŏgi, then move the right foot to the L₂ direction. | Oen-twitku-bi | Kŭmgang-momt'ong-makki |
| 15 | Keeping both feet fixed. | Oen-twitku-bi | Tanggyŏ-t'ŏkch'igi |
| 16 | Keeping both feet fixed. | Oen-twitku-bi | Orŭn-chumŏk-yŏp-chirŭgi |
| 17 | Lift the right foot up to assume the Hakdari-sŏgi with left foot. | Oen-hakdari-sŏgi | Oen-toltchŏgwi |
| 18 | With the left foot fixed, execute the Yŏpch'agi with right foot so that the right foot lands to the front (L₂ direction). | Orŭn-apkubi | Oen-p'algup-p'yojŏk-ch'igi |
| 19 | Move the right foot toward the left and the Moa-sŏgi move | Orŭn-twitku- | Sonnal-momt'ong-makki |

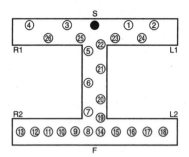

| | the left foot to the S direction. | bi | |
|---|---|---|---|
| 20 | With the left foot fixed, move the right foot one step forward (S direction). | Orŭn-apkubi | P'yŏnsonkkut-sewo-tchirŭgi |
| 21 | Using the right foot as the axis, trun the body to the S direction. While turning, place the right arm behind the back and move the left foot forward. | Orŭn-twitku-bi | Oen-dŭngchumŏk-ŏlgul-pakkat-ch'igi |
| 22 | With the left foot fixed, move the right foot one step forward. | Orŭn-apkubi | Mont'ong-pandae-chirŭgi |
| 23 | Using the right foot as the axis, turn the body to the left while moving the left foot to the L1 direction. | Oen-apkubi | Kawi-makki |
| 24 | With the left foot fixed, execute the Apch'agi with the right foot so that the right foot lands to the front. | Orŭn-apkubi | Momt'ong-tubŏn-chirŭgi |
| 25 | Using the left foot as the axis, turn, the body to the right while moving the right foot to the R1 direction. | Orŭn-apkubi | Kawi-makki |
| 26 | With the right foot fixed, execute the Apch'agi with left foot so that the left foot lands to the front (R1 direction). | Oen-apkubi | Momt'ong-tubŏn-chirŭgi |
| Kŭman | Using the right foot as the axis, turn the body to the left, and while moving the left foot. | Naranhi-sŏgi | Kibon-chunbi |

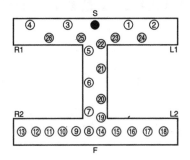

# TAEKWONDO TERMINOLOGY

## A

| | |
|---|---|
| Anmakki | Inside block |
| Anp'almok | Inside forearm |
| Apch'agi | Front kick |
| Apch'igi | Front strike |
| Apkubi | Forward stance |
| Apsŏgi | Front stance |
| Arae-makki | Low block |

## C

| | |
|---|---|
| Ch'agi | Kick |
| Ch'aryŏt | Attention |
| Ch'aryŏt-sŏgi | Attention stance |
| Chebip'ŭm-mokch'igi | Swallow shape neck strike |
| Chech'yŏ-tchirŭgi | Upper thrust |
| Ch'igi | Strike |
| Chirŭgi | Punch |
| Chuch'um-sŏgi | Riding stance |
| Chumŏk-chirŭgi | Fist punch |
| Chunbi | Ready |
| Chunbi-sŏgi | Ready stance |

## H

| | |
|---|---|
| Hakdari-sŏgi | Crane stance |
| Hanbon-kyŏrugi | One step sparring |
| Hech'yŏ-makki | Scattered block |
| Hoshinsul | Self defence |

## K

| | |
|---|---|
| Kkoa-sŏgi | Cross stance |
| Kŭmgang-makki | Diamond block |
| Kŭp | Color (yellow, blue, red) belt |
| Kyŏkp'a | Breaking |
| Kyŏngnye | Bow |
| Kyŏrumsae | Sparring stance |

## M

| | |
|---|---|
| Makki | Block |

| | |
|---|---|
| Mechumŏk | Hammer fist |
| Moa-sŏgi | Close stance |
| Mok-ch'igi | Neck strike |
| Momt'ong-tchirŭgi | Trunk thrust |
| Momt'ong-makki | Trunk block |
| Murŭp-ch'igi | Knee strike |

**N**

| | |
|---|---|
| Naranhi-sŏgi | Parellel stance |
| Nullŏ-makki | Press block |

**O**

| | |
|---|---|
| Oen | Left |
| Oesant'ul-makki | Part mountain shape block |
| Orŭn | Right |

**P**

| | |
|---|---|
| Pakkat-makki | Outside block |
| Pakkat p'almok | Outside forearm |
| P'algup-ch'igi | Elbow strike |
| P'almok | Forearm |
| Pandae-chirŭgi | Reverse straight punch |
| Paro-chirŭgi | Straight punch |
| Pat'angson-nullŏmakki | Palm hand press block |
| Pŏm-sŏgi | Tiger stance |
| Pochumŏk | Covering fist |
| P'um | Red/black belt, Finished Movement |
| P'umsae | Pattern |
| P'yojŏk-chigi | Target strike |
| P'yojŏk-chirŭgi | Target punch |

**S**

| | |
|---|---|
| Sabŏmnim | Instructor |
| Santŭl-makki | Mountain shape block |
| Sewo-tchirŭgi | Vertical thrust |
| Shihap | Competition |
| Sonnal-ch'igi | Hand-knife strike |
| Sonnal-momt'ong-makki | Hand-knife trunk block |
| Sonkkŭt-tchirŭgi | Spear hand thrust |

**T**

| | |
|---|---|
| Tan | Black belt |
| Tanggyŏ-t'ŏkch'igi | Jaw strike |
| Tŭngchumŏk | Back fist |
| Tobok | Taekwondo uniform |
| Tojang | Practicing hall |
| Toltchŏgwi | Hinge shape |
| Tollyŏ-ch'agi | Turn kick |
| Tongmilgi | Push barrel |
| Tti | Belt |
| Twihuryŏ-ch'igi | Back hook kick |
| Twitch'igi | Back kick |
| Twitkubi | Backward stance |

**Y**

| | |
|---|---|
| Yŏpch'agi | Side kick |
| Yŏp-makki | Side block |

# REFERENCES

*Dictionary of Korean Myths and Symbols*, Seoul: Dong-A Publishing, 1992

Kim, Sang-il. *Hanism as Korean Mind.* Seoul: Onnuri Publishing, 1993

*Kukkiwon Taekwondo Text Book*, Seoul: Ohsung Publishing, 1989

Lee, Kyong Myong & Nowicki, Dariusz. *Taekwondo.* Warszawa: Alma Press, 1988

Lee, Kyong Myong. *Richtig Taekwondo.* Munich: BLV Sportspraxis, 1987

Lee, Kyo Yoon. *Taekwondo Textbook*, Seoul: Chang-jin Publishing, 1994

Lee, Kyong Myong & Chung, Kuk Huung. *Taekwondo Kyorugi.* Hartford: Turtle Press, 1994

WTF. *Taekwondo Handbook, 1994 Edition*

WTF. *International Referee Seminar Texbook, 1990 Edition*

Kim, Sang Hwan. *Ultimate Fitness Through Martial Arts,* Hartford: Turtle Press, 1993